L

Original Text by James P. Reza
and Matthew R. Poole
Updated and edited by Martha Ellen Zenfell
Cover photograph by Catherine Karnow
Layout Concept: Klaus Geisler
Managing Editor: Tony Halliday

Berlitz POCKET GUIDE

Las Vegas

11th Edition 2003

Photography by: Las Vegas News Bureau/Las Vegas Convention & Visitors Authority except pages 11, 15, 33, 34, 35, 40, 41, 60, 61, 63, 66, 69, 73, 81, 99 by Matthew R. Poole/Las Vegas Convention & Visitors Authority; 12, 47, 51, 76, 77, 86, 100 by Glyn Genin; 21 by Topham Picturepoint; 13, 34 by Bellagio; 50 by the Neon Museum; 56 by the Liberace Museum; 67 by Al Seib; 72 by the Riviera, 79 by the Mirage

Contacting the Editors

Every effort has been made to provide accurate information in this publication, but changes are inevitable. The publisher cannot be responsible for any resulting loss, inconvenience or injury. We would appreciate it if readers would call our attention to any errors or outdated information by contacting Berlitz Publishing, PO Box 7910, London SE1 1WE, England.
Fax: (44) 20 7403 0290;
e-mail: berlitz@apaguide.demon.co.uk

Printed in Singapore by Insight Print Services (Pte) Ltd, 38 Joo Koon Road, Singapore 628990.
Tel: (65) 6865-1600. Fax: (65) 6861-6438

The fountains in front of Bellagio make this lavish casino-resort a Vegas attraction that should not be missed (page 35)

The Guggenheim Hermitage brings classy culture to Las Vegas from this house of excellence in art (page 58)

See Vegas Vic and the Fremont Street Experience (page 45) for neon nirvana

TOP TEN ATTRACTIONS

The sphinx and the pyramid are the amazing highlights of the Luxor (page 28)

The Grand Canyon (page 66) is one of the wonders of the natural world, and is just an excursion away from Vegas

Fine dining reaches new heights in Vegas. Picasso (page 107) not only offers wonderful cuisine, but you can sit right next to world-class art

Thrill seekers shouldn't miss the Big Shot at the Stratosphere (page 44)

Desert Passage (page 34) offers a unique retail therapy experience, complete with indoor 'rainstorm'

Hoover Dam is a 1935 marvel of engineering (page 61)

Downtown gambling is the bargain of the baize, and Binion's Horseshoe (page 50) is among the best

CONTENTS

Fact Sheets

MGM
LUXOR

LAS VEGAS AND ITS PEOPLE

Only 100 years ago, this city of mythic proportion and impossible illusion was no more than a dusty railroad stop in the middle of an unforgiving desert valley. Dramatic changes occurred in the valley throughout the 20th century to create this fantasy, known today as the 'Entertainment Capital of the World.'

Initially settled in the mid 1800s, Las Vegas struggled as a Mormon outpost for much of its early existence. The site was only declared a town in 1905. That year, on May 15, officials from the San Pedro, Los Angeles & Salt Lake Railroad auctioned 1,200 parcels of land mapping 40 square blocks in the desert dust. Within a year, the city's population had grown to 1,500 brave pioneers.

A newly-released Frank Sinatra song, *It's Time for You*, was the centerpiece of a $13 million Las Vegas promotion.

Landmarks of the Modern World

Today's visitors are greeted by the fastest-growing, most rapidly changing city in the American West. They mingle and play among iconic landmarks of the world's great cities. Replicas of the Eiffel Tower, the skyscrapers of Manhattan, the palaces of ancient Rome, and an Egyptian pyramid loom to entrance and entice.

Modern visitors see no trace of the features that spawned and nurtured the fledgling city – its natural springs – most of which have long since run dry. Though water flows freely through the artificial lakes, lush resort swimming areas, and sprinklers for the famous golf courses, it now comes in a giant pipeline from the Colorado River. Without that pipeline, the city would dry up and crumble back into the desert.

The extraordinary Blue Man show at the Luxor

Fast Lane

Las Vegas is located in Clark County, Nevada, near the southern tip of the state. Clark County has about 1.3 million inhabitants, and roughly one third of them are residents living in Las Vegas. Nevada, ranking as the seventh largest state in the union by area, has a total of almost 2 million inhabitants, making it the 32nd most populous state. The population of retired people is growing four times as fast as in the rest of the United States, and for four decades in a row Nevada has been the fastest-growing state in America.

Sunny Days

Las Vegas has an average of just four inches (10cm) of rainfall and more than 250 days of sunshine each year. Summers are hot, with temperatures often nearing 115°F (46°C). In

World Capital of Boxing

Las Vegas probably has a better claim than any city to the title of 'the World's Capital of Boxing.' Vegas is often the promoters' choice as the venue for major title bouts, including world championships.

Sonny Liston, Muhammad Ali, Leon Spinks, Larry Holmes, Mike Spinks, George Foreman, and Evander Holyfield are just a few of the fighters to have won the heavyweight championship title in Las Vegas. After his retirement from the ring, Joe Louis stayed on and was popular as a greeter at Caesars Palace.

winter, daytime temperatures can be a pleasant 65°F (18°C), but nights are cold. Early spring and late fall are the best times to visit, as the days are warm and the nights comfortably cool.

The fuel that builds and runs all of Las Vegas

Rush to the New

Las Vegas is unfettered by the burdens of history or preservation. Old buildings or resorts simply give way to the pressures of age or fashion and are remodeled, or, at the extreme, imploded, accompanied by fireworks and street-wide celebration. Few remember, or perhaps even care, that the Italian-themed Venetian is on the site of the Sands – the Rat Pack's most famous haunt. Today, Italy; tomorrow France in Steve Wynn's new Le Réve casino. After that, who knows?

Las Vegas, like a gambler, has often reinvented itself. After the Mob era, Sin City became a family-friendly destination and it is now beginning yet another phase as a top-notch resort city. Today's Las Vegas has world-class accommodations, five-star dining, and shopping that rivals any major city, added to the town's reputation for all-night gambling, drinking, and adult-oriented diversions. Hotel-casinos have positioned themselves as complete resorts, offering full-service day spas, huge shopping malls, and attraction-filled theme parks – all in addition to the gam-

New York-New York; it's one heck of a sight

bling, golf courses, and showrooms. Newer resorts, like Bellagio, aim to recapture the glamor of the Rat Pack era. Always betting on growth, expansion, and the power of positive cash flow, Las Vegas has transformed itself once again.

Reinvention

Such rapid change and reinvention results in what many call a city without a soul. But for over one million residents and 30 million annual visitors, this characteristic – the city's instinct for the next big thing – makes Vegas the city of their dreams. In fact, many come as visitors and choose to stay. For nearly a decade, almost 4,000 have become new residents each month, pushing the population of the valley up by nearly 1,000 percent since that first railroad auction.

Outside the resort corridors, new suburban residential developments swallow the surrounding desert, edging to the bases of the mountain ranges east and west. Unlike the original American suburbs, new master-planned communities like Summerlin and Green Valley are thriving cities within themselves. New businesses spring up almost immediately, built into the plan and ready to serve an already-waiting community of clients. Driving through these areas feels like a ride through a movie set – the homes are sparkling and modern, the highways smooth and wide, and the landscaping young, fragile, and new.

Local Las Vegas

Driving in the central city, within a few miles of Downtown, are the plaster-walled and wood-floored houses of Charleston Heights and the Huntridge and, nearby, the city's first upscale developments, Rancho Circle and the Scotch 80s. Here, just a short way from the crowds and lights of Fremont Street and Glitter Gulch, are quiet, ranch-style homes complete with swimming pools, tennis courts, horse corrals, and lush, mature landscaping. Also beyond the Strip and Downtown lie other indications of a living and breathing metropolis.

The University of Nevada-Las Vegas mentors a student population of over 23,000, although, like most people in Las Vegas, they are commuters through the endless gridlock that now defines the streets. Before the recent rapid expansion, the city claimed to have more churches per capita than any other in the United States. Spiritual guidance was apparently a pressing need for the dwellers on the excessive fringes of temptation.

Siegfried & Roy, with magicians in the making

Although Las Vegas is still dominated by the gambling industry, non-gaming business flourishes here as well, thanks to the county's and state's favorable tax structure. Much of the non-gaming business is in suburban business parks and master-planned communities, an effort to reinvent the metropolis with industrial and commercial centers across the valley. Credit-card companies and banks, mail order firms, health care subsidiaries, and software developers are all in the economic mix. They help Las Vegas to diversify, as the national attitudes to gambling shift like the desert sands.

Las Vegas shows new sprouts of cultural growth, too. Local theater is healthy, a first-class public art museum recently opened, and the Guggenheim museums have brought world-class art collections to an eager public.

Spectacular Sports

For athletic visitors and locals, too, one of the attractions of this city in the desert is its easy access to sports. Whether watching from a ring-side seat as great events unfold, like a Mike Tyson heavyweight boxing championship, or showman Evel Knievel jumping over a canyon in his 'Skycycle,' to taking active advantage of the golf, hot-air ballooning, tennis, hiking, or canoeing possibilities, nothing is far away. Nor are some of the most important wonders of the world, whether they be natural – like the Grand Canyon and Death Valley – or man-made, like the very impressive Hoover Dam.

Get hitched in the shadow of the Stratosphere Tower

The fabulous fountains of Bellagio

Las Vegas' shows – musical, magical, or just totally theatrical – are among the best in the world, employing the finest of Hollywood muscle to build state-of-the-art performance arenas that encourage extravaganzas to reach new heights. And while Sin City confronts the same issues that face all growing cities – crime, the problems of growth and expansion – Las Vegas continues to amply demonstrate just what a 21st-century megalopolis can accomplish.

Glittering Moments

Las Vegas's transformation from a watering hole – via a gambling way-station to a desert retreat for Hollywood heavyweights, and now, to an international resort city – have all been whistle-stops on the city's journey of evolution. This city with eyes firmly on the future can never be dull, and attracts tourists in their millions to the Las Vegas lifestyle, if only for a few glittering moments.

A BRIEF HISTORY

The inhabited history of the Las Vegas Valley has been traced to 23,000 BC, when much of the area was covered by a prehistoric sea. The people of the time lived in caves, hunting mammals that gathered at the shoreline. The landscape of the valley changed dramatically over the next 200 centuries. The glaciers feeding the lake melted and the lake evaporated. Fossils tell a story of man's slow development.

First Inhabitants

Around 3000 BC, native Archaic people began the development of a lasting hunter-gatherer culture. By this time, the valley was geographically similar to how it is today, with the exception of artesian springs bubbling to the surface. The springs fed a network of streams, draining through the Las Vegas Wash to the Colorado River. Surrounding the springs were desert oases, sprawls of grasses, trees, and wildlife. Many of the springs crossed the center of the modern Las Vegas metropolitan area.

275 million years ago, the Mojave, Great Basin, and Sonoran deserts formed the floor of a great inland sea.

For about 4,000 years, the Archaics, in a culture with many signs of early civilization. Further advancement appeared halfway through the first millennium AD, with the arrival of the Anasazi people. More progressive than the Archaics, the Anasazi used agricultural techniques like irrigation to nourish their crops. The Anasazi reached a benchmark of advanced society – living in permanent shelters year-round, without the need to follow wildlife. Mysteriously, the Anasazi vanished from the valley around AD 1150, leaving it to be repopulated by another hunter-gatherer tribe, the Southern Paiutes. Un-

Native American pictographs in the Valley of Fire State Park

skilled in the agri-techniques of the Anasazi, the Paiutes were semi-nomadic until European settlers arrived and changed the cultural landscape of the valley.

From Mailmen to Mormons

In the early 19th century, America's western territories were still largely unexplored. It was not until 1829 that Rafael Rivera, a Mexican scout, found a spring-fed valley and dubbed it '*Las Vegas*' – a Spanish name that leaves many modern visitors wondering exactly where 'the meadows' really are.

For 15 years, Las Vegas was used as a Spanish Trail way-station. In 1844, American explorer John C. Fremont parked his horses at Big Springs, and his report to the government resulted in a mail route leading past the spot on its way to California. This put Las Vegas on the map and was one of the crucial turning points of its history. In 1855, Mormon leader Brigham Young responded to promising reports of this oasis by sending 30 missionary settlers to the valley; they eventually built a fort near today's downtown area. Surrounded by farmland hewn from the hard desert, this adobe fort was the center of Las Vegas' development for 50 years. The missionaries struggled valiantly against the harsh desert, trying to both survive in the terrain and spread the Mormon faith. But pressures from arriving miners pushed the missionaries' plight beyond recovery. Their supplies scarce, their harvest meager, and their spirit broken, they abandoned the fort in 1858.

Although the local land was rich in silver, by 1865 most of the mining traffic through Las Vegas was of prospectors headed to California or Northern Nevada in the quest for gold.

Explorer John C. Fremont

Las Vegas Ranch

One opportunist who stayed was Octavius Decatur Gass. Having plenty of the pioneer spirit that characterizes Las Vegas to this day, Gass picked up where the Mormons left off, with ranching and farming. He took over the abandoned fort and 640 acres (260 hectares) surrounding it, naming it the Las Vegas Ranch. He expanded the ranch and irrigated the land to support crops and cattle. Gass became a Justice of the Peace and a territorial legislator, but despite his ambition, his success was short-lived. In the late 1870s, he defaulted on a loan from rancher Archibald Stewart, and Stewart took the Las Vegas Ranch for his own. True to Wild-West stereotypes, Stewart was slain by a neighboring farmer, leaving the ranch to his strong-willed wife, Helen. Through 1905, Helen Stewart expanded the ranch to 2,000 acres (810 hectares), making herself quite a bit of money in the process.

What happened next would mark the end of the successful Las Vegas Ranch and the beginning of the era of the subdivision seen across almost all of western America to this day. The railroad was coming, and when it arrived, Las Vegas would never be the same again.

Of Tracks and Tracts

At the turn of the 19th century Los Angeles and Salt Lake City were among the burgeoning metropolises of the new American West. When the two cities were linked by rail, the Las Vegas Valley (which at the time had a non-native population of less than 30) changed again.

Native Americans inhabited the Las Vegas Valley for about 5,000 years. First came the so-called Archaics, then, around 300 BC the Anasazi, and more recently the Paiutes.

In 1903, officials of the San Pedro, Los Angeles & Salt Lake Railroad arrived in Las Vegas, eager to secure a right-of-way for their Los Angeles–Salt Lake connection. Las Vegas would serve as a major stopover for crew rest and train repairs. For all this, the railroad needed land. As mapped, the track traveled directly through Helen Stewart's Las Vegas Ranch, so Stewart sold 99.5 percent of her ranch to the railroad. The remainder she returned to the native Paiutes.

The route between Los Angeles and Salt Lake City was completed in 1905 and railroad tracks bore right into the center of the Las Vegas Valley. On May 15, 1905, the railroad held a land sale – a milestone in Las Vegas history. Standing at the depot at Main and Fremont streets, officials auctioned 1,200 lots, subdivided from 40 square blocks of desert scrub. Land speculators and locals alike were anxious for a part of the newest railroad boomtown, and more than 80 percent of the lots were sold that afternoon.

Las Vegas was no longer a small pioneer settlement. With rail service in place and 40 blocks of private property, it was ready to become a real town. Businesses sprang up overnight, and wooden houses were erected to replace the tent city where many of the early settlers lived. One short year after the auction, the population of Las Vegas had swelled to 1,500 residents.

Mayme Stocker, the wife of a railroad man, was granted the first Las Vegas gambling license. She opened the first casino, The Northern Club, on Fremont Street in 1920.

Dam Good Luck

From the beginning, Las Vegas had served travelers, first on the Spanish or Paiute Trail, then the mail route. Now the railroad needed a way station, and Las Vegas was the place. By 1915, after 10 years of growth, the town had telephones, 24-hour electricity, and a growing population – many of whom worked in the railroad repair shop.

With growing competition in rail transport, Union Pacific bought the Los Angeles–Salt Lake line. Union Pacific then consolidated its operations, eliminating the Las Vegas repair facility. Las Vegas had been incorporated into Nevada's new Clark County in 1909, when the legislature also outlawed gambling. These circumstances threatened to relegate Las Vegas to the status of a small desert community struggling to support its 3,000 residents. But the Southwest's growing need for water, combined with fortuitous proximity to the

Las Vegas shortly after the construction of the Hoover Dam

Colorado River, would give Las Vegas a second chance of prosperity. Construction on the Hoover Dam (originally called the 'Boulder Dam,' and later renamed for the president who authorized it) began in 1931, in a canyon 45 miles (72km) southeast of Las Vegas.

Bringing $165 million to the southwestern economy, the Hoover Dam prevented Las Vegas from drying up, financially and literally. The project brought jobs and created Lake Mead, the massive reservoir that provides the water for the whole of southern Nevada.

Public Relations

The construction of the Hoover Dam wasn't Las Vegas' sole savior, however. The state legislature helped too, legalizing gambling in 1931 and securing the future of the town. The hordes of people who attended the dam's 1935 dedication set the city's now-formidable public relations machine into action. They went to work on what has become one of the lengthiest tourism campaigns ever attempted. The city soon established itself as a Wild-West town with an 'anything goes' attitude. Vices outlawed or heavily controlled elsewhere were legal here, at any hour of any day or night. So began Las Vegas's reputation as an adult theme park.

Further fuel for the valley's economy came with World War II. The Las Vegas Aerial Gunnery School, now Nellis Air Force Base and the Nevada Test Site, in the north, and Basic Magnesium in nearby Henderson, grew from America's war effort. By 1945, the population had grown to almost 20,000, with workers and airmen moving in at a pace.

Gambling, and the Rat Pack

Gaming thrived Downtown in the 1930s and early 1940s, and casinos emerged on the stretch of the old Los Angeles Highway now known as the Strip; El Rancho Vegas was the first, in 1941. Then a new migrant came onto the Strip – the

The Mob in Vegas

In 1946, Benjamin 'Bugsy' Siegel opened the Flamingo, an opulent resort on the southern end of the LA Highway. His vision was Hollywood flair, the new Vegas flash with Mob money. But the Mafia bosses weren't pleased with its performance and Siegel was murdered in the summer of 1947. Despite its initial failings, Siegel's Flamingo survived him, as did Mob infiltration of casinos.

Money from the Teamsters Union was used to fund the Stardust and other casino operations; the unions' total investment in Las Vegas was shown to exceed $238 million. Law enforcement investigations, beginning with the hearings of Tennessee Senator Estes Kefauver in 1950, took until the late 1960s to make a serious impact on the influence of organized crime in the Las Vegas gaming business.

Robbie the robot takes to the tables, 1957

Mob *(see page 20)*. From the mid-1940s to the mid-1960s, emerging stars came to Las Vegas with dreams of making it big: Frank Sinatra, Wayne Newton, and Louis Prima among them. The Rat Pack – originally Frank Sinatra, Dean Martin, Sammy Davis Jr, Peter Lawford, and Joey Bishop, made legendary appearances at the Sands in January 1960, including filming the original *Ocean's 11*. To capitalize on the increasing popularity, more casinos emerged along the Strip, including the Desert Inn, Sahara, Sands, and Riviera.

New Legitimacy

In the 1960s, organized crime met a formidable rival for control of Las Vegas – corporate cash. First came the arrival in 1966 of billionaire Howard Hughes. As a recluse and an invalid, Hughes was borne on a stretcher to the Desert Inn's penthouse. Six weeks later he was asked – then instructed – to vacate the suite for the high rollers who had previously booked it. Hughes immediately bought the Desert Inn and fired the management. During his three-year residence, he never once allowed cleaners into the suite, and he saw no-one face to face except for his bodyguards. Yet Hughes' $300-million Las Vegas buying spree took in many properties along the Strip, plus plots of land from the Strip to the mountains.

Hughes' influence would have beneficial repercussions, both immediate and lasting. Because of the legitimacy Hughes conferred by investments, established companies such as Hilton Hotels bought into the gaming business, and their influence drew a line in the desert sand between lawful operations and Mob casinos, where illegal skimming of profits was rife. That, and the formation of the Nevada Gaming Control Board, helped turn the tide against Mob influence in the city.

Las Vegas with a Vision

The legitimization of gambling led to disorganization and reassessment. The competition forced casino operators to look again at their business models and their markets. Leading the way was Steve Wynn, a Vegas resident and owner of the Golden Nugget casino. In the mid-1980s, Wynn began to reinvigorate the Strip.

Howard Hughes stayed in Las Vegas for almost exactly three years. In that time he bought the Desert Inn, Landmark, Frontier, Silver Slipper, and Sands casinos, three more parcels of land on the Strip, an airline, and a TV station. According to legend he bought the TV station just so he could choose the late-night films that they aired.

He bought several key properties there – the Silver Slipper and Castaways among them – and demolished them to make way for a new kind of resort. The Mirage was an instant suc-

Elvis and Priscilla at their Vegas wedding in 1967

cess. Wynn's demolition of existing properties started a trend that led to many more implosions. The Dunes was replaced by Bellagio, Aladdin by the new Aladdin, and the Sands made way for the Venetian. Wynn's casinos have also set new standards of fantasy – Excalibur, the MGM Grand, the Luxor, and New York-New York all followed Mirage's lead during the 1990s, offering themed environments and family attractions.

The Modern Era

By the middle of the 1990s, the new approach brought a backlash; visitors found the Las Vegas experience was becoming mediocre. In response, new resorts started to offer attractions and amenities modeled after top worldwide resorts, including luxurious spas, signature restaurants, and exclusive boutiques.

A handful of these resorts – such as the South-Seas themed Mandalay Bay, the Venetian, and the Four Seasons – now market themselves squarely at the luxury travel market. The crème de la crème of Vegas deluxe is Bellagio. The world's most expensive resort to date at $1.6 billion, Bellagio's amenities include five-star dining, high-caliber boutiques, and world-class art exhibitions. High-end accommodations have raised expectations back to the glamorous mythology of the Rat Pack era.

City of the Future

As it changed from Mob gambling town to corporate gaming venue, the population of Las Vegas skyrocketed. Over 20,000 additional hotel rooms have been added in a few short years, including resorts in Summerlin and Lake Las Vegas. Recent projections for Las Vegas predict challenges; tourism revenues must increase substantially to sustain what is already built, while figures show visitor numbers as steady or declining. The growth that has characterized Las Vegas for nearly a century could be heading for a roadblock.

Still, the future is sure to be in the pioneering spirit that built the city from a few springs in the desert to the fantasy that it is today. With its new image repositioned, its good looks glittering, and its careful aim in sight, Las Vegas seems worth a pretty good wager.

A vision of the modern city is Paris Las Vegas

Historical Landmarks

1150 Paiute Indians inhabit Las Vegas Valley, replacing the Anasazi.
1829 Scout Raphael Rivera discovers springs in the desert and names the land 'Las Vegas,' which is Spanish for 'the meadows.'
1844 Explorer John C. Fremont camps at Las Vegas Springs, on a site that later bears his name, Fremont Street.
1848 The US acquires the region after winning the Mexican War.
1855 Mormon settlers build an adobe fort to protect the mail route.
1905 The San Pedro, Los Angeles & Salt Lake Railroad makes an inaugural run and auctions lots in a new town called Las Vegas.
1931 Construction of the Hoover Dam commences.
1931 Gambling is legalized in Nevada.
1941 El Rancho Vegas is the first casino to open on the stretch of Los Angeles Highway that later became known as the Strip.
1945 The population of Las Vegas reaches 20,000.
1946 Benjamin 'Bugsy' Siegel, a member of the Meyer Lansky crime organization, opens the Flamingo Hotel.
1960 The Rat Pack shows, with Frank Sinatra, Sammy Davis Jr, Dean Martin, Peter Lawford, and Joey Bishop, sell out the Sands.
1966 Howard Hughes' arrival at the Desert Inn heralds the new corporate era of Las Vegas gaming.
1975 Nevada gaming revenues top $1 billion.
1980 Las Vegas (population 164,674) celebrates its 75th birthday.
1989 Steve Wynn opens the Mirage casino with 3,039 rooms.
1990 Las Vegas' population reaches 258,295.
1994 Work begins Downtown on the Fremont Street Experience.
1995 A monorail starts up between the MGM Grand and Bally's, on the east side of the Strip. The Fremont Street Experience opens.
1999 Mandalay Bay, New York-New York, and Paris Las Vegas open.
2000 The Venetian opens with over 3,000 suites.
2001 Steve Wynn implodes the Desert Inn to make way for Le Réve.
2002 Despite opposition, the Federal government plans to ship nuclear waste to Yucca Mountain, 100 miles (160km) north of Vegas.

WHERE TO GO

Since Bugsy Siegel's Flamingo Hotel set a new standard in 1946, nothing in the world rivals the Las Vegas Strip's audacity or the casinos' desire to outdo each other. This 3½ mile (5.5km) section of the old Los Angeles Highway is both famous and notorious for its extravagant recreation. Stretching from the Mandalay Bay resort in the south to the Stratosphere Tower to the north, this portion of Las Vegas Boulevard South has evoked more melodrama and mythology than the rest of the city combined.

Las Vegas may be the only place on earth where architects work to make buildings seem smaller than they are.

Miles of neon tubing and millions of dazzling incandescent and fiber optic lights illuminate every hour of darkness year-round, while casinos that never close leave the doors to their comfortably air-conditioned interiors wide open, even while the summer sun burns down at 115°F (46°C). The excess is staggering, but visitors come to play and partake from all the far corners of the world.

Glittering Playground

A cornucopia of resorts, stores, restaurants, and – of course – glittering casinos line both sides of the thoroughfare, tantalizing onlookers. Dozens of the world's largest hotels are congregated directly around the action, simply because the hotels *are* the major attractions. Some of these mega-resorts revel in the clichés of the past, while others offer a chic opulence that borders on the unreal. Roman palaces, the Eiffel Tower, the pyramids of Egypt, and the jungles of Polynesia all await anyone with a yen to indulge in the extravagance, and a bankroll to withstand the trip.

THE STRIP – SOUTH

At the southernmost end of the Strip is the **Mandalay Bay Resort and Casino**. The $950-million behemoth has over 5,000 rooms, including a unique 'hotel-within-a-hotel': opulent rooms managed by the Four Seasons group *(see below)*. Central to Mandalay's jungle-city theme is an 11-acre (4.5-hectare) tropical environment, complete with a wave pool that beats upon a sandy beach. Also featured are a House of Blues restaurant and club, a 1,700-seat showroom, a 12,000-seat arena, a convention center, and a spa. Mandalay's excellent restaurants include Aureole, China Grill, Wolfgang Puck's Trattoria del Lupo, and the vodka bar Red Square.

> **The Sphinx in front of the Luxor casino is able to project an enormous hologram with laser beams set in its eyes. The trick was stopped when airplane pilots in the sky complained.**

The Four Seasons company, renowned for its superlative attention to guests' needs (poor customer service is a major complaint at most Las Vegas resorts), offers one of Las Vegas's only non-gaming resorts within the Mandalay Bay, the **Four Seasons Hotel Las Vegas**. A total of 424 ultra-luxury rooms and suites occupy floors 35 to 39 of the Mandalay Bay tower, reachable only via a private elevator in the Four Seasons' lobby. A separate driveway leads to a two-story main building housing four restaurants and bars, a health spa, and meeting rooms. A huge pool set in a lush garden is available only to hotel guests. If your priorities are for comfort first and gambling second, the Four Seasons Hotel is for you.

Next up along the Strip is the mighty black peak of the ➤ **Luxor Hotel and Casino**, 30 stories of tinted glass and steel topped with a night-defiant shaft of light, visible by air from Los Angeles (they say). Encompassing the world's largest

Egyptian facade of the Luxor

atrium, the pyramid (and its two adjoining towers) house over 4,000 rooms and a stunningly huge casino, lavishly decorated with *faux* Egyptian artifacts. There are other attractions worth noting, though, including the Oasis Spa, Ra nightclub, a 3-D IMAX movie theater, 12 restaurants, and a motion-simulator ride. One of the biggest thrills for guests of the hotel is the ride to the bedroom on the 'inclinator,' an elevator that moves up and sideways at the same time.

Tropicana

The smallest and oldest of the four resorts at the busy intersection of Las Vegas Boulevard and Tropicana Avenue, the **Tropicana Resort and Casino** ignored the family-aimed marketing of the 1990s and held pretty tightly to the notion of Las Vegas as an adult escape. The main showroom's *Folies Bergères* has wooed audiences with its topless showgirls since 1961. The understated class of the hotel tower may have lost some luster but still retains an air of respectability, while the tropical pool area (with swim-up blackjack tables) is nearly perfect. The **Casino Legends Hall of Fame** (open: daily 9am–9pm) claims to be the largest collection of gaming memorabilia ever assembled, and is well worth visiting.

Excalibur

One of the first resorts with a theme, the **Excalibur Hotel and Casino** is a Medieval Faire aimed squarely at families and travelers on a budget. This is evident in the execution – though in no way shoddy, the overall experience is cheap and cheerful. For a brief period, the Excalibur was the largest hotel in the world, though its 4,008 rooms were soon surpassed by the MGM Grand. One of the best attractions is *King Arthur's Tournament*, a live re-creation in a showroom of a Middle Ages jousting tournament, and one of the few dinner shows left in Las Vegas. The 100,000-sq-ft (9,300-sq-m) casino caters mostly to minimum betters, with $3 blackjack tables and nickel and dime slot machines. The resort, like most of Las Vegas, is definitely seen at its best in the night-time – viewed from the Strip, the brightly illuminated spires and battlements are a fine sight.

Medieval fantasy at Excalibur

New York-New York

The MGM lion

Taking theme hotels to a new level, the **New York-New York Hotel and Casino** actually spawned lawsuits by Manhattan architects. Its dozen towers are uncanny, one-third-size replicas of famous New York skyscrapers, including the Empire State Building, the New York Public Library, and the Chrysler Building. Inside, the detailed illusion continues with cartoon quality, such as the fake subway station complete with graffiti, Coney Island arcade, and 84,000-sq-ft (7,812-sq-m) casino area fashioned after Central Park – right down to the trees, footbridges, and street lamps. The Greenwich Village dining environment nearly overshadows the food, but the Motown Cafe offers treats for your musical palate. The Empire Bar is a classy after-hours spot, and the **Manhattan Express roller coaster** is worth the wait.

MGM Grand

Across the Strip, the **MGM Grand Hotel and Casino** is so massive – the casino floor is the size of four American football fields – that most visitors become completely disoriented as they wander the resort. Past guests may remember the overly cute Wizard of Oz theme, which has been replaced in a multi-million-dollar renovation by a new, more mature style incorporating MGM's most famous movies. How big is big? Try 5,034 guest rooms spread across 114 acres (46 hectares), 12 restaurants (including establishments by Wolfgang Puck, Emeril Lagasse, and Mark Miller), an elaborate 6½-acre (3-hectare) pool complex, a spa and tennis facility, three arenas, a comedy club, and the Studio 54 nightclub. There are four gaming areas, each with a different theme, and minimum bets ranging from $5 to $500, as well as nearly 4,000 slot machines and lively sports betting. The adjoining 18-acre (7-hectare) theme park, once open to the public, is now used for special functions only. High rollers may be offered accommodations in one of 30 private villas at The Mansion. Like most casinos, the MGM Grand now operates loyalty-card-style schemes for players to accumulate perks, known locally as 'comps.'

Monte Carlo

The **Monte Carlo Hotel and Casino** evokes a classic Las Vegas atmosphere, remarkably accessible to any traveler. Striking in its elegant European theme, this resort has an understated style rare in modern Las Vegas. In homage to tradition, the resort offers a wide range of gaming, dining, retail, and spa amenities. Though it looks like a haven for high rollers, minimum bets are actually quite modest, starting at

Slot Machines

Slot machines generate two-thirds of Nevada casinos' take, with the nickel slots producing $1 billion annually. Today, slots take up 60 percent of casino floor space and generate more profits for the casinos than from all table games combined. Currently, casinos average about 3,000 slots apiece. The programming of the machines makes a jackpot rare enough for the big pay off, but still allows for a tidy profit for the casino. Most machines are set to pay out somewhere between 83 and 98 percent, but slot payoffs vary from one casino to another.

The phenomenal popularity of slot machines may be because they require no skill, and the pace can be set by the player. Players are driven by the idea that a machine will be ready to pay off after a certain amount of play, though payouts are more likely to be random.

The Monte Carlo has an understated style

$5; they even have 5¢ slots. The **Lance Burton Theatre** showcases the entertaining and amusing act of this classic Las Vegas performer, who has been bewildering audiences with his magic tricks since 1991.

Anyone who craves the familiarity of a hotel chain will like the **Holiday Inn Boardwalk**. Rates are higher than Holiday Inn's usual charges, but this *is* the Strip, after all. Despite a few Coney Island-like attractions, there is no real theme to the hotel.

Aladdin

Across the street is the new **Aladdin Hotel and Casino**. Out went the 1960s Aladdin and in came the 21st-century version. The original played host to the 1967 wedding of Elvis and Priscilla Presley, in the private suite of the then- owner, Milton Prell. The newer Aladdin Hotel and Casino continues the long-running theme of Middle Eastern fantasy and legend. The hotel offers seven restaurants, a showroom, and a performing arts theater. Adjoining it is the **Desert Passage** shopping promenade, fabulously arranged with Moorish architecture, good stores and an indoor tropical rainstorm. If walking the many miles of shopping aisles has made your feet tired, simply hail a cart and be pedaled by a muscular youth to one of the arcade's 14 restaurants.

Paris Las Vegas

The **Paris Las Vegas Hotel and Casino** took the theme concept to new levels with this massive $750-million, 2,900-room hotel-casino, modeled after the Hôtel de Ville in Paris. The property is a Vegas-style homage to the city of romance, complete with Arc de Triomphe. Patrons can see the bright city lights from the top of the one-half scale Eiffel Tower, go shopping on the Rue de la Paix, or dine in one of eight

The conservatory at Bellagio

Parisian-inspired eateries, including a restaurant in the tower itself. Cobblestone walkways lead to other landmark replicas, among them the Paris Opera House and the Louvre. After 11pm, you can even arrange for a wedding ceremony at the top of the tower. Be prepared for high minimum stakes in the gilded casino, however, where gaming opportunities include more than 2,000 slot machines.

The iridescent glass sculpture over the lobby at Bellagio cost over $10m. It was made by Dale Chiluly, the first American accepted by the Italian glassmakers of Murano, near Venice.

One of the old guard of Las Vegas resorts, **Bally's Hotel and Casino** has eschewed transformation over the years. Despite the $14 million futuristic light-and-water show out front, Bally's is an exercise in classic Las Vegas style. Inside, all is comfortable and inviting, with dark colors and grand chandeliers hanging above the casino floor. Since Bally is the leading maker of gaming machines, you'll find all the latest video versions of poker, blackjack, craps, and roulette (a great place to learn how to play). The showroom features the adults-only *Jubilee!*, while headliners have included everyone from Penn & Teller to Paul Anka. Try the pricey but luxurious Sterling Brunch. Behind the casino is a monorail running to the MGM Grand.

Bellagio

The most lavish resort in Las Vegas is the **Bellagio Hotel and Casino**, a stunning replica of an Italian villa that boasted an equally stunning price tag: $1.6 billion dollars. Gaming rooms offer an unlikely quiet elegance, while the **Gallery of Fine Art** (open: Sun–Thur 10am–6pm, Fri, Sat until 9pm) hosts traveling exhibitions. The dining is unparalleled, as are the luxurious accommodations, with more on the way in a new tower. The conservatory features a dazzling display of flowers, which change with the seasons. Also worth a look is the spectacularly choreographed water show in the small lake fronting the resort, as well as Cirque du Soleil's remarkable aquatic show called *O,* although tickets don't come cheap and are booked out way in advance. One caveat: shopping in the hall of retail fame that is Via Bellagio is for big spenders. Tiffany and Prada have stores here, and it is fun to browse.

Caesars Palace

➤ A standard-setter since its 1968 opening, **Caesars Palace Hotel and Casino** is one of the few old-timers to keep pace with modern Las Vegas, perhaps because its ancient Rome theme was popular from the outset (that, and the genuine marble never seems to go out of style). Here, elegance seems within anyone's reach, though having lots of money certain-

The Flamingo has a desert oasis theme

ly helps. The casino is a high-roller's heaven with lofty limits at many tables. Sports fans will enjoy the lively environment at the Sports Book, where bets are placed on athletic events. Additional pleasantries include a fitness center and a spa. The popular and respected **Forum Shops** offers a fabulous spread of shopping, as well as dining for any budget, while the Omnimax Theatre and IMAX 3-D motion simulator ride, both located in the Forum Shops, are very popular with kids of any age.

Caesars Palace

Tiny by Strip standards, but occupying a powerful corner of the famed boulevard, the 200-room **Barbary Coast** begs the question: 'How and why has it survived?' The rooms offer a charming and comfortable rendition of 1900 San Francisco, but a real draw of the hotel-casino is the recently added restaurant, Drai's. Already recognized as one of Las Vegas' best, Drai's arrived when Hollywood restaurateur Victor Drai took over the hotel's basement offering his own vision of the nouvelle French menu.

THE STRIP – NORTH

Parts of the northern Strip glitter less brightly than its southern neighbor, but there is still plenty to see and do. The **Flamingo Hilton Las Vegas** retains Bugsy Siegel's original theme of a 'desert oasis' with a lush tropical pool and garden area complete with swans, ducks, penguins, and flamingos; otherwise, little of the older hotel survives. Amenities range from nine restaurants to five pools, six tennis courts, a newly renovated health club, and several pricey boutiques. Most gaming tables offer low minimum bets, however, and slot junkies have a choice of more than 2,000 machines waiting to be fed.

Adjacent to the Flamingo Hilton is tiny **O'Sheas Casino,** intimate, somewhat cozy and easily overlooked amid the colossal resorts around it. Although the charming Magic & Movie Hall of Fame is now permanently closed, the prominent sign remains to tantalize, as it is the subject of a historic preservation order.

Imperial Palace

Recognizable by the blue-neon tinted pagoda architecture that stands apart on the Strip, the sprawling **Imperial Palace Hotel and Casino** houses 2,700 rooms, 10 restaurants (including two buffets), and a 75,000-sq-ft (6,975-sq-m) casi-

The daily pirate battle at Treasure Island

no. Aside from the gaming room, the most popular draws here are the *Legends In Concert* impersonation show and the **Imperial Palace Auto Collection** (open: daily 9:30am–9:30pm), where collectable and historic automobiles are displayed. Check out Marilyn Monroe's convertible.

The pioneer of modern themed resorts, the **Mirage Hotel and Casino** shows some age when compared against the newer extravaganzas. Still, it is attractive to both high- and low-rollers, owing to a lush environment (think Maui on steroids) and stylish accommodations. The pool area is particularly pleasant. The minimum bets here are steep, starting at $5 for blackjack and roulette, but there is plenty of free quality entertainment once you've blown your gambling budget. The Lagoon Saloon features live music in an indoor rain forest, while nine restaurants feed the hungry masses with everything from buffet fare to gourmet cuisine. Left of the check-in desk is an incredible and mesmerizing aquarium. The big attractions here are the Siegfried & Roy magic show, the Dolphin Habitat, the Secret Garden, and the White Tiger Habitat. Fronting the hotel is the famous Mirage volcano, belching flames and water to delight pedestrians.

The Treasure Island sea battle, the Mirage's erupting volcano, and the fountains of Bellagio draw crowds that stop traffic. This is one reason the LVPD are so tough on jay-walkers.

Harrah's

Harrah's Las Vegas underwent a $200-million renovation in the fall of 1997 that changed it from a Mississippi riverboat theme to a trite *Carnival* motif – a transformation that has few critics cheering. A profusion of bright colors, fiber-optic fireworks, and huge murals of international fêtes tends to put visitors on festivity overload. It's a sizable establishment, with over 2,600 guest rooms and a 103,000-sq-ft (9,579-sq-m) gaming area. Seven restaurants, including the popular Range Steakhouse, offer a welcome respite from the glitz. The real fun is in The Improv comedy room.

Treasure Island

Treasure Island offers yet more affordable elegance. This hotel appears much like its sister resort, the Mirage, but the $430-million Treasure Island is the lower-budget of the two, though not in quality. Eighteenth-century Caribbean pirate exuberances – carved ceilings, dark woodwork, brass adornments – are everywhere. As in the Mirage, betting limits start at $5 and quickly rise as the sun sets. Outside, a sea battle stops pedestrian traffic, raging nightly between a pirate ship and a British frigate. Inside, Cirque du Soleil's show *Mystère* takes the circus to new levels of sophistication. The pirate theme may appeal to children, but this is mostly for adults – the kids will have a better time at Circus Circus.

Gondoliers were recruited from the ranks of boatmen in Venice, Italy, to ply the Venetian's Grand Canal at the casino's opening.

➤ The **Venetian Resort Hotel-Casino**, on the site of the former Sands hotel, pushes the Italian-theming envelope. Renaissance Venice is evoked with dramatic replicas of the Doges Palace, Campanile, and canals with gondolas and serenading gondoliers. The resort's capacity of 3,000 rooms has recently been expanded with the construction of another tower. The entertainment plaza includes a showroom, but the real centerpiece is the **Grand Canal Shoppes**, a collection of upscale stores and restaurants.

Fans of Country & Western will like the **New Frontier Hotel and Casino**. Elvis Presley played his inaugural Las Vegas show here in 1956, proving that the New Frontier is

Circus Circus is fun for families

not too new after all. Built with a Wild-West motif long before the themed resort era, the hotel is small by modern standards (a 'mere' 986 rooms). Amenities are spare – four restaurants and a pool, but the huge casino offers plenty of good elbow room.

The Desert Inn, a Las Vegas classic, was imploded in 2001 to make room for Steve Wynn's newest $1.6 billion fantasy, **Le Réve**. Inspiration came from a Picasso masterpiece, *Le Réve*, which Wynn happens to own. The casino is due to open in 2004. A part of the Desert Inn was retained and now houses an art exhibition, the Wynn Collection.

Circus Circus

First of the family-friendly low-roller casino some two decades ago, **Circus Circus Hotel and Casino** shows signs of fatigue. The renovated lobby is classy, but Strip hotel rooms aren't this cheap without some compromise. Howev-

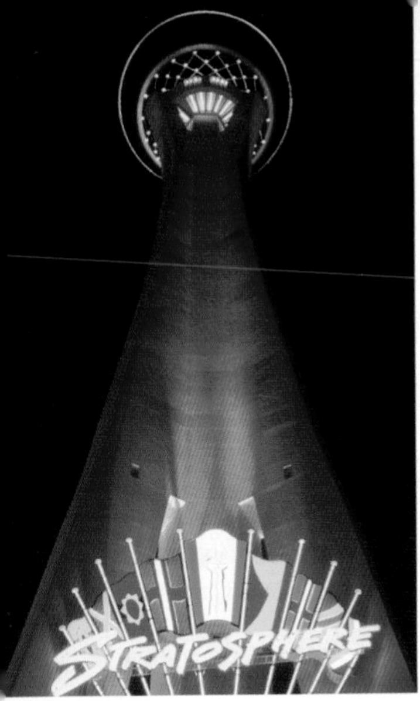

The Stratosphere Tower at night

er, families still appreciate the free circus acts every half-hour from 11am to midnight, as well as the carnival games, arcade, and the giant indoor amusement park, **Adventuredome**.

The huge casino area is separated into three areas, connected by walkways and a monorail. To watch the circus acts, just look up from your slot machine. Compared to the rest of the Strip, the Circus Circus is a throwback that attracts low-rollers looking for cheap thrills. Kids will also enjoy the **Guinness World of Records Museum** (open: daily 9am–5pm), next to Circus Circus, which features extraordinary items aplenty.

The Stardust

But hey, time to forget all that 'family experience' stuff – the **Stardust Resort and Casino** is a dandy adult-oriented gambling playground. The Stardust is geared toward anyone seeking the basics: gaming, liquor, food, and topless showgirls. The casino includes state-of-the-art sports betting and 2,000 slot machines, as well as $1 blackjack tables. There are six restaurants, and eight separate bars handle the liquor output. The **Wayne Newton Theater** showcases its perennially popular namesake – with shows six nights of the week.

When it opened in 1955, the nine-story **Riviera Hotel and Casino** was the Strip's first high-rise, styled after the luxury resorts of the Côte d'Azur. The days of Liberace and Orson Welles gracing the showroom are long gone, and today's Riviera attracts a less stellar clientele. Piecemeal expansion has left a confusing layout. There are 2,100 guest rooms, and restaurants include the upscale Kristofer's Steakhouse. There are swimming pools, tennis courts, and a small shopping area, but the real attractions are the adult live shows. Some showgirls are partly immortalized by a sculpture of bronzed bare rear-ends.

The Sahara

Built in 1952, the **Sahara Hotel and Casino** underwent a $100-million renovation, transforming it to a themed Moroccan palace. The renovation replaced the dark and plush atmosphere with a lighter decor, and the result has been one of comfort, suitable for tour groups, conventioneers, and mid-budget travelers. Close to 2,000 rooms and 75,000 sq ft (6,975 sq m) of gaming surround a beautiful pool area. The **Sahara Speedworld** offers Indy-car racing simulation, but skip the buffet, which does not get high marks. Though the casino area is not elegant, the minimum limits are as low as $1, and the pit bosses can be more relaxed and good-humored than elsewhere on the Strip.

The Sahara, a favorite on the Strip since 1952

The **Stratosphere Hotel and Casino** and its soaring **Stratosphere Tower** struggle against the challenges of location – too far north for the Strip, too far south for Downtown, The complex sports a faint World's Fair theme, but it's definitely a vast improvement over Vegas World, the universally loathed hotel it replaced. The hotel's centerpiece is the 1,149-ft (350-m) tower, which includes a 109th-floor observation deck (the highest in the US), an 83rd-floor revolving gourmet restaurant, and two thrill rides (the **Big Shot** is truly a frightening experience).

Along with the requisite gaming area – which is well thought of for its loose slots and low-limit tables – are seven restaurants, over 40 stores, and the *American Superstars* impersonator show. Skip the expensive taxi ride from the lower Strip and hail one of the free shuttles.

DOWNTOWN

While the Las Vegas Strip eclipsed the draw of Downtown early in the city's history, the charm of Glitter Gulch is not lost for many who visit. Both the city's oldest casino (El Cortez) and its oldest hotel (the Golden Gate, where Las Vegas's first telephone was installed) are located Downtown, as are numerous other properties, including magnate Steve Wynn's first, the Golden Nugget.

Until recently, Fremont Street was Las Vegas's civic gathering spot, home to holiday parades and the Wild-West-themed Helldorado festival. Additionally, there was once a thriving local shopping and business area here, home to Sears, J.C. Penney, and numerous law and medical offices. Over time, the shopping moved to the sub-

Two million light bulbs and 208 loudspeakers deliver the 100-ft (30-m) spectacle of the fabulous Fremont Street Experience. The moving picture show features jet fighters, exotic birds, and dancing girls.

The Fremont Street Experience uses 2 million light bulbs

urbs and the attorneys moved to high-rise offices just outside the gaming area. Recently, in the face of stagnating Downtown revenues, local government and business owners have tried to explore ways to increase traffic to the famed district.

Fremont Street Experience

The **Fremont Street Experience** (shows every hour, starting at dusk), was the first of these experiments, the combined project of casino owners and the city. In 1995, Fremont Street (between Las Vegas Boulevard and Main Street) was closed to traffic and landscaped into a pedestrian mall, but the real draw of the $70 million attraction is the 90-ft (27.5-m) high vaulted canopy that covers this four-block stretch. Covered with over 2 million lights that dance to a 540,000-watt sound system, all controled by computer, the Experience features a regular parade of amazing audio-visual shows that really wake you up. Aside from making the area more friendly, the Experience also cleaned up the Downtown city blocks – at least the part under its influence. The Experience has now been joined by a non-gaming entertainment complex called **Neonopolis**. Opened after much delay in 2002, the $99-million complex features the 16-screen Crown Movie Theaters, restaurants, shopping, and underground parking, with lots more to come.

The Fremont Street area is a throwback to the old days of Las Vegas gaming. House gambling rules are generally more flexible, allowing for both lower minimum bets and higher limits (sometimes even no-limit gaming). Additionally, there is a certain rough quality to Downtown, an experience different than that offered at the shiny new Strip resorts. Do not mistake this edginess for danger; the Fremont Street Experience has done quite a bit to improve the safety of the area beneath the canopy, sometimes drawing the ire of civil rights and free speech activists. Darker reaches off the beaten track of central Downtown are still considered hazardous for tourists, though.

Main Street Station and the Plaza

Main Street Station is perhaps Las Vegas's best-kept secret. Just north of the Fremont Street Experience, this Victorian-styled casino fulfills the promise of the exterior architecture and gas-fired street lamps with an astoundingly detailed interior filled with valuable antiques. Unlike other casinos, Main Street showcases genuine articles; a carved Scottish fireplace and Teddy Roosevelt's Pullman car among them. Dining includes the upscale Pullman Grille for steak and seafood, and the Triple 7 Brewpub for handcrafted ales and wood-fired pizza.

The monorail that will link casinos on the Strip is planned to eventually reach all the way to Downtown's city blocks.

The neon **Plaza Hotel and Casino** – located at the west end of the Fremont

The Plaza, Golden Gate, and Las Vegas Club casinos

Street Experience canopy – has a smoky, 1970s feel, and has always been a maverick of the hotel-casinos. With just over 1,000 rooms and a 75,000-sq-ft (6,975-sq-m) gaming area that includes penny slots, the Plaza attracts an interesting mix of friendly gamblers and seniors. The showroom offers campy, adult-oriented revues.

Hotel California

The name of the **California Hotel and Casino** is misleading. The people who run this off-Fremont Street hotel-casino on Ogden Avenue spend most of their marketing budget in Hawaii, attracting islanders by the planeload who provide up to 85 percent of the casino's business. Consequently, the theme is the South Seas, and the four restaurants feature Hawaiian dishes and drinks. There is a Hawaiian specialty gift store for souvenirs, and 781 modestly priced rooms aimed at the budget traveler.

Lady Luck

The **Lady Luck Casino Hotel** on North Third Street is a collection of neon, mirrors, and brass, going a long way toward preserving the glitzy Las Vegas of old. Close to 800 rooms are very comfortable, especially the ones in the two newer towers. The hotel-casino offers two facilities that are scarce Downtown: a showroom, staging a production magic show, and a swimming pool. Four restaurants serve guests, including the gourmet Burgundy Room, a member of the exclusive Chaîne des Rôtisseurs association.

The **Las Vegas Club Hotel and Casino**, one of the oldest casinos in Las Vegas, marks the beginning of the Fremont Experience canopy. Explore 40,000 sq ft (3,720 sq m) of gaming with some of the most liberal house rules in town. The modest theming here features a widely dispersed exhibition of sports memorabilia, as well as card dealers dressed in jersey-like uniforms. The hotel tower was added in 1980 and features 410 affordable, comfortable rooms. There are also three casual restaurants.

Exhibited at the Gold Nugget is the world's largest gold nugget. Found in Australia, it weighs 59.84lb (27.2kg).

Perhaps the only bed-and-breakfast experience in Las Vegas, the San Francisco-styled **Golden Gate Hotel and Casino** has stood at One Fremont Street since 1906. The charming operation is the city's oldest hotel, the home of its first telephone, and the original purveyor of the classic shrimp cocktail. Its 106 small but elegant rooms with plaster walls and mahogany doors hark back to another era, and its coffee shop is an unusually classy Downtown experience. Piano players entertain with infectious ragtime.

The only prominent Downtown hotel-casino without a multicolored neon sign, the 1946 **Golden Nugget**, was remodeled as Steve Wynn's first hotel project in 1987. Metropolitan

The Golden Nugget is one of Downtown's classiest casinos

elegance supersedes the surrounding glitz. Guests, greeted by uniformed doormen, enter a gilded lobby full of marble and crystal. The guest rooms and misted pool area landscaped with palms are fancy enough to have earned top ratings. The Golden Nugget showroom offers headliners and production shows; there are five restaurants as well, including a top-notch mid-priced buffet and two gourmet dining rooms.

4 Queens

A blinding neon landmark since 1966, the **4 Queens Hotel and Casino** today mainly attracts older guests, many of whom are repeat customers. A 12-seat blackjack table (the world's largest) and a giant slot machine draw players to the 60,000-sq-ft (5,580-sq-m) casino. The 700 rooms of earth-tone decor are pleasant and affordable. Its four restaurants include Hugo's Cellar, an always-busy classic Las Vegas gourmet room with a winning wine list.

A sign from the Neon Museum

Fitzgerald's Casino and Hotel is the Las Vegas low-rollers' gaming haven. Once the tallest building in Nevada at 34 stories, Fitzgerald's 650 rooms offer terrific views of the city and the mountains. Accommodations are of the national chain-hotel variety, and priced accordingly, ie, not expensive, as are the numerous restaurants and bars.

Binion's Horseshoe

Founded by gambler Benny Binion, **Binion's Horseshoe Hotel and Casino** may be the most traditional, old-school gaming joints left in town. Flocked wallpaper and velvet drapes decorate the gaming room with the highest betting limits in town, and no-limit gaming. Additionally, the Horseshoe hosts the annual $1-million **World Series of Poker**. The Binion family are ranchers, and premium beef can be had in both the casual coffee shop and the upscale Ranch Steak House.

The **Fremont Hotel and Casino** was one of Las Vegas' first high-rises, built in 1956, and is famous for launching Wayne Newton's career. The hotel no longer has a showroom, but 452 modest guest rooms accommodate the Hawaiian travelers who frequent the place. The Fremont's block-long signage helps turn Downtown night into day, and the Second Street Grill is a hidden gem, featuring Pacific Rim specialties.

As Las Vegas experienced record growth and continued a trend toward the implosion of its older resorts, a desire arose to preserve some of the city's history. Neon signage is perhaps the single most recognizable icon of Las Vegas. So, the **Neon Museum** has assumed the responsibility of raising funds to restore some of the rusting signs from the past and display them in their glory. Recently, signs were installed on posts in the Fremont Street area and around Neonopolis, as the Neon Museum itself has no permanent premises.

El Cortez

Unrivaled for its continuous parade of low-stakes gamblers and their related chums, **El Cortez Hotel and Casino** (built in 1941), is the city's oldest operating casino. Unabashedly proletarian, the gaming area is filled with smoke and the cheap perfume worn by the ragtag old-timers who frequent its slot machines. The relatively large 80,000-sq-ft (7,440-sq-m) casino features absurdly low limits, while dining rooms offer ridiculously cheap food. Semi-annual lotteries based on social security numbers are held for $50,000 prizes. There are 402 rooms at low prices; in the tower, you will get a bit more than you pay for.

Vegas Vicky, Fremont St icon

SoHo in the Desert

Local culture can be sampled at the **Arts Factory** complex (tel: 702-676 1111, open: Mon, Tues, Thur, Fri noon–5pm), located on East Charleston Boulevard. An old warehouse converted into artists' studios, this place is a touch of SoHo in Sin City and the lynchpin of

Elvis-A-Rama, the official Las Vegas shrine to the King

a growing Downtown arts scene. Inside are fun commercial and not-for-profit galleries that exhibit avant-garde art in the **Contemporary Arts Collective** (tel: 702-382 3886); local artists in the **Smallworks Gallery** (tel: 702-388 8857); and more mainstream arts in the **George L. Sturman Fine Arts Gallery** (tel: 702-384 2615). Call to check current opening hours.

WEST OF THE STRIP

Las Vegas has been described as 'Des Moines with casinos,' and to a certain extent that is true – beyond the glitter of the Strip, the quality of attractions pales somewhat. But there are still intriguing stops worth a visitor's time and effort. And while most hotel-casinos and resorts are concentrated along the Strip and within the Downtown area, some are found just off the Strip. To the west are recently developed resort corridors off both Flamingo Road and Tropicana Avenue.

These areas consist primarily of light industrial development with sparse housing or apartments nearby. To the east of the Strip is the convention area of Paradise Road, offering – in addition to traditional hotel-casinos – a spate of non-gaming business-oriented hotels as well as a developing restaurant row. Here are some of the highlights of these properties and attractions to the West of the Strip.

➤ **Elvis-A-Rama** (3401 South Industrial Road, tel: 702-309 7200, open: daily 10am–6pm) will even appeal to those who aren't fans of The King. Elvis imitators pop up everywhere in Vegas, but on display here are some geniune articles, including a 1955 Cadillac the singer bought with his signing fee from RCA.

Three different kinds of casinos are located on West Flamingo Road. The **Rio All-Suites Resort and Casino** offers such a variety of quality mid-priced amenities that it has received international acclaim. A recent addition raised the room total to 2,556, and the standard accommodations are among the city's largest. Also added were **Masquerade Village** – a Carnivale-themed collection of gaming, retail outlets, and restaurants (including Napa, one of Nevada's best) – and the **Voodoo Lounge**, a top-floor cocktail lounge with citywide views. The casino floor, lorded over by serious-looking pit bosses wearing laughably gaudy tropical wear, is packed with locals and tourists, especially on weekends. Five-dollar minimum bets are standard. After the night's last performance, the showroom becomes the Club Rio disco for late-night dancing.

The Rio All-Suites Resort

The Palms

When **The Palms** opened in 2001, it was the first new hotel in 15 months, a lifetime in the city's frenzy of endless novelty. With an understated Polynesian theme, the hotel is decorated in soft beiges and taupe. Check out the stylish **Ghost Bar**.

Gold Coast and Orleans

Offering a combination of entertainment and gaming, the **Gold Coast Hotel and Casino** fulfills many traditional Las Vegas expectations. On site is a 72-lane bowling center, a lounge with karaoke, and a dance hall that regularly features live big-band, swing, and rockabilly music. Dining rooms are varied, inexpensive, and good, while a twin theater (with unbelievably cheap concessions) screens an alternating parade of blockbusters and festival films. The true casino draw is in the huge number of video poker machines, which attract mainly locals, despite the 740 hotel rooms.

The showy facade of the **Orleans Hotel and Casino** on West Tropicana Avenue, is a bit misleading and overbearing; once you enter, the decor is rather subtle. The casino is more akin to a warehouse than the Big Easy, but the 50-ft (15-m) ceilings do well to eradicate the typical smoky, claustrophobic atmosphere. A 72-lane bowling center and 12-screen movie theater attract locals, while the eight casual restau-

Conventions

Despite the size of the Las Vegas Convention Center, many conventions spill over to adjacent hotels, particularly the Las Vegas Hilton. COMDEX and the Consumer Electronics Show – in the fall and winter – especially tend to sprawl. Other major conventions include gatherings of the construction industry, automobile accessory marketers, fashion companies, and even pizza-equipment industries.

The obvious financial benefit of the influx of conventioneers is offset by snarled traffic, inflated room rates, and packed attractions. Some merchants – and most taxi drivers – complain that conventioneers are less free-spending than vacationers. Still, city planners continue to woo the convention trade by expanding its main convention center and adding new ones throughout the valley.

The Las Vegas Convention Center

rants and 827-seat showroom (staging second-tier or aging acts) attract anyone seeking quality on a budget. Rooms are spacious and among the city's best bargains.

EAST OF THE STRIP

For all its reputation as a vacation hot-spot, Las Vegas has also enjoyed tremendous success as a major convention destination. Every week companies, industries, and lifestyle organizations arrive en masse from all over the world to mix business with pleasure. How vital are such trade shows to the city economy? Enough so that most Las Vegas resorts have elaborate convention facilities, as do suburbs such as Henderson.

The king, however, is the **Las Vegas Convention Center**. This complex ranks as the largest single-story convention floor in the United States, and – what's more – is constantly being expanded. It is also within walking distance of more than 50,000 hotel rooms, one of the center's main attractions.

The **Las Vegas Hilton Hotel and Casino** – next to the Convention Center – is perfect for lovers of large-scale resorts catering to every need. Public areas are graciously decorated and there are 3,174 plush guest rooms. Amenities include a spa, six lighted tennis courts, 12 restaurants, and a showroom and lounge featuring top talent. Hilton highlights are a huge sports betting floor, *Star Trek: The Experience*, a permanent high-tech attraction featuring futuristic gaming, dining, and its centerpiece interactive amusement ride. Proximity to the convention building means the Hilton's occupancy and rates rise during conventions, so book in advance.

Liberace Museum

Liberace may no longer be with us, but Mr Showmanship's absolutely fabulous cars, gilded pianos, and indescribable costumes can still be seen at the **Liberace Museum** on East

The Liberace Museum is a study in excess

Tropicana Avenue (tel: 702-384 3466, open: Mon–Sat 10am–5pm; Sun 1–5pm). The jewel of the entertainer's collection may in fact be a fake jewel – a 50-pound rhinestone, said to be the world's largest. This shrine to one of America's most popular and campiest pianists won't disappoint.

The Hard Rock

The Hard Rock

One of the more notable hotels in Las Vegas not located on the Strip is the **Hard Rock Hotel and Casino** on Paradise Road. A surprising exercise in casual elegance, considering its theme, this experiment a few years ago, aimed at the younger market, has resulted in a rebirth of the glory days of Vegas. If you're wondering where many of the hip and pretty people hang out, this is it. Guitars of the stars and other music memorabilia are on display, as in all the Hard Rock restaurants. Hardwood flooring surrounds the handsome casino – slot machine handles, for example, are shaped like Fender Stratocaster guitar necks – while performers of every musical style attract full houses in the 1,200-seat club-style showroom. Dining includes the trendy Mr Lucky's 24/7 and the upscale Mortoni's. A lush pool area greets sunbathers, and rooms are spacious and tasteful. Expansion has doubled the property's amenities, but has not destroyed the hotel's reputation.

CULTURAL ATTRACTIONS

Las Vegas is gunning hard to establish itself as a center for the arts, but even though the city's history is short, its past is not being neglected. There are several institutes devoted to

Shark exhibit at the Lied Discovery Children's Museum

Las Vegas history, including the **Nevada State Museum and Historical Society** on Twin Lakes Drive (tel: 702-486 5205), and the **Clark County Heritage Museum** on South Boulder Highway (tel: 702-455 7955). The state museum has a woolly mammoth display, of the variety that used to live in Nevada. The very good **Las Vegas History Museum** (900 Las Vegas Boulevard North, tel: 702-384 3466) is large on reptiles and snakes. Visitors to the **Old Mormon Fort Historic Park** (southeast corner of Las Vegas Boulevard and Washington, tel: 702-486 3511) can see remnants of the city's oldest building, a fort built by original Mormon settlers in 1855. All four museums are open daily 9am–4pm. There's plenty to engage adults, too, at the **Lied Discovery Children's Museum** (833 Las Vegas Boulevard North, tel: 702-382 3445, open: Mon–Sat 10am–5pm, Sun 1–5pm).

Guggenheim Hermitage

At the Venetian is one of the classiest museums in the US, the **Guggenheim Hermitage Museum** (tel: 702-360 8000, open: daily 9am–11pm). The Guggenheim Hermitage, in conjuction with the prestigious Russian museum of the same name, showcases great masters on the theme 'Art Through the Ages.' Its sister establishment, Guggenheim Las Vegas, opened with the glamorous 'Art of the Motorcyle,' a huge success in New York (the town, not the casino), but unfortunately was forced to close its doors in early 2003. Across

Twain Avenue from the Venetian is the **Wynn Collection** (tel: 702-733 4100, open: daily 9am–11pm), where paintings by Van Gogh, Cézanne, Pisarro, and Renoir are exhibited. It's located through the lobby of the old Desert Inn.

Across town on West Sahara Avenue is the **Las Vegas Art Museum** (tel: 702-360 8000, open: Tues–Sat 10am–5pm, Sun 1–5pm). The museum, attached to the Sahara West Library, is large and designed to the exacting specifications of the Smithsonian Institute. Curators schedule a mix of local and touring shows, often including work by recognized masters.

The University of Nevada, Las Vegas

The **University of Nevada at Las Vegas** (UNLV) and the **Community College of Southern Nevada** have been unofficial outposts of beyond-the-neon culture since their in-

The Art of the Motorcycle opened Guggenheim Las Vegas

ception. UNLV's sprawling urban campus on South Maryland Parkway has quite a collection of interesting sights and venues. The **Marjorie Barrick Museum** (tel: 702-895 3381, open: Mon–Fri 8am–4:45pm, Sat 10am–2pm) is a natural history museum with live lizards, gila monsters, tortoises, and a red snake, as well as stuffed birds. There are also some excellent exhibits on the arts and crafts of the Paiute, Navajo, and Mexican Native Americans.

Just outside the entrance is the campus **Xeric Garden**, a landscaped sampling of desert plants in a beautiful setting. The **Donna Beam Fine Arts Gallery** (tel: 702-895 3893, open: Mon–Fri 9am–5pm, Sat 10am–2pm) is a spacious hall exhibiting the work of students as well as professionals. Also on campus is the **Artemus Ham Concert Hall** (tel: 702-895 3801), featuring classical, rock, and theatrical performances, and the **Thomas and Mack Center**, an 18,000-seat arena

Lake Mead is perfect for outdoor recreation most of the year

hosting everything from hockey to rodeos and musical events. On the Community College campus at 3200 East Cheyenne Avenue, the city's only **planetarium** (tel: 702-651 4759) features nightly shows of both Omniscreen films and programs about the heavens. Telephone for information.

The great Hoover Dam, completed in 1935

EXCURSIONS

Hoover Dam and Lake Mead

There is much to do within easy driving distance of Las Vegas, from recreation to sightseeing. Easily the top draw is the **Hoover Dam**, responsible for Las Vegas's first major crowd (of 20,000), who attended its 1935 dedication. Long after its completion, the dam remains an awe-inspiring sight, living up to its old billing as the 'Eighth Wonder of the World.'

Striking sculptures by Oskar J.W. Hansen may be the largest monumental bronzes ever cast in the US. A dizzying 725ft (526m) high, this engineering marvel straddles the Nevada-Arizona border a half-hour's drive south of Las Vegas on US93. The Hoover Dam Visitors Center is open daily from 8am to 6pm, tel: 702-294 3524, but the last tour is around 4pm. Since the September 11, 2001 disaster, the tours inside the dam have been suspended, but a two-hour discovery tour has been introduced for the one million visitors who come here each year.

The man-made result of Hoover Dam, **Lake Mead** offers more than 500 miles (800km) of shoreline in the midst of a 1.5-million-acre (607,000-hectare) national recreation area.

Angling at Lake Mead

A popular spot for locals and visitors alike, America's largest man-made body of water is open all year (peak usage month is June). Activities include swimming, boating, fishing, water-skiing, self-guided hiking, camping, and picnicking. Boats can be rented at the **Lake Mead Marina** or the **Echo Bay Marina**. The *Desert Princess*, a Lake Mead Cruises paddle-wheel boat, offers breakfast and dinner cruises (tel: 702-293 6180). The company schedules trips around the lake on Jet Skis, as well as a fast-paced jet-boat excursion that heads in the direction of the Grand Canyon. The lake is best reached through Boulder City, a half-hour drive south of Las Vegas.

Boulder City

Boulder City itself is an anomaly in Nevada – a city that rejects gaming and discourages excess growth. Its small-town feel is quaint and charming by the standards of booming suburban southern Nevada. The heart of the town is a historic square, fronted by 1930s-era buildings such as the **Boulder Dam Hotel** and the **Boulder Dam Theatre**. The hotel houses several galleries, stores, and an attractive restaurant, while the town is home to several art galleries and antiques shops; call the Chamber of Commerce, tel: 702-293 2034 for details. Also worth seeing is the **Hoover Dam Museum** (tel: 702-294 1988, open: daily 10am–5pm, Sun noon–5pm), which is well-stocked with artifacts from the building of the dam and the founding of Boulder City. In the fall, several festivals, including Art in the Park and Damboree (a celebration of the town's heritage), entice thousands to abandon the gaming tables and make the trek from Las Vegas. Take US93 south about 25 miles (40km) from Vegas; Hoover Dam is an additional 7 miles (11km).

Ghost Towns

While not really a ghost town, **Goodsprings** has the feel of a genuinely spooky place. The functioning homes are surrounded by mill foundations and abandoned mine operations. The hamlet's chief attraction is the popular Pioneer Saloon, the country's largest stamped-metal building. Head south from Las Vegas on Interstate 15 and turn at the tiny town of Jean. The true and authentic ghost town of **Rhyolite** is located 126 miles (200km) northwest of Las Vegas on US95. Once Nevada's second-largest city, thanks to a 1904

Red sandstone illuminates Valley of Fire State Park

Calico Ghost Town, near Barstow in California, has been restored as a themed amusement park where visitors can take train rides and see silver-mine tunnels.

gold strike, remnants can be seen in the Tonopah–Las Vegas Railroad depot. A top attraction is the 'bottle house,' built of 50,000 glass bottles, common practice in the days of scarce building supplies. Just outside town is an unlikely cluster of large Belgian sculptures including Albert Szukalski's *Last Supper* (a re-creation of the da Vinci masterpiece using plaster ghosts as the Disciples), a 28-ft (8.5-m) miner, and a 25-ft (7.5-m) female nude built of cinder blocks.

Valley of Fire State Park

Fifty miles (80km) northeast of Las Vegas via Interstate 15 (watch for the Valley of Fire exit, State Route 169), **Valley of Fire State Park** is a spectacular alien landscape of erosion-sculpted, brilliant red sandstone. The park features Native petroglyphs dating to 300BC, most accessible by light hikes. Atlatyl Rock has a stairway to the carvings, while the glyphs at Mouse's Tank require an easy quarter-mile (0.5-km) trek. For the car-bound, there is a 6-mile (9.5-km) scenic loop through White Domes, a stunning vista of sandstone formations that were once the bottom of an inland sea. There are also some picnic areas and overnight campgrounds. The park is best visited in late spring or fall.

Red Rock Canyon

➤ **Red Rock Canyon National Conservation Area**, a half-hour drive west of downtown Las Vegas via Charleston Boulevard, is a dramatic vista of mountains and colorful sheer rock faces. In reality more than just a single canyon, it is a 13-mile (21-km) ridge with canyons eroded into its flanks. First stop should be the Red Rock Visitors Center (tel: 702-363 1921, open: daily until 4:30pm), which has archaeological displays and dioramas depicting the lives of the early native inhabitants who lived here. At Willow Spring, well-preserved petroglyphs can still be seen.

Scenic Loop

Starting at the center, the scenic loop meanders through the area's stunning topography, but when driving on the loop, watch out for bicyclists. Picnicking spaces are plentiful, as are hiking trails of varying levels of difficulty. During migratory seasons, bird watchers can have a field day. The canyon is one of the nation's top rock-climbing sites, with an almost endless variety of ascents, but novices should stick to an appropriate level; rescuers are frequently called out to help find lost or injured visitors.

The Bighorn sheep is one of Nevada's most important animals

Mount Charleston

For a cool break from the desert, try 11,918-ft (3,632-m) **Charleston Peak**, near the town of **Mount Charleston**, 40 minutes north of Las Vegas on US95. Two areas command particular attention: Kyle Canyon and Lee Canyon. Kyle is home to scenic Cathedral Rock, Mary Jane Falls, and Big Falls, all accessible by trail (Cathedral Rock requires a three-hour trek). Lee Canyon is home to a ski and snowboarding resort, remarkable for being so near the desert. The mountain features numerous scenic overlooks and picnicking sites, while the ranger station on Kyle Canyon Road can provide advice.

Grand Canyon

There are several noteworthy national parks within driving distance of Las Vegas. The most famous and most popular is the ➤ **Grand Canyon**. The North Rim is 280 miles (448km) east of Las Vegas; the South Rim 260 miles (416km) from Vegas. There are no connecting bridges across the divide. The South

Grand Canyon

One of the world's most spectacular natural phenomena, the Grand Canyon averages 10 miles (16km) wide and reaches depths of 5,700ft (1,700 m). It passes through five of the seven temperate zones, and each has its own unique ecology. Declared a National Park in 1919, the canyon was 'discovered' by Lieutenant Joseph Ives in 1857, who called it a 'pointless locality.'

The canyon has been created over millions of years by the erosion of the great Colorado River. From the lookout points at the rim of the canyon, the river seems little more than a trickling stream. Climbing within designated areas is encouraged: strata of red-and-yellow sandstone sandwich layers of dark granite and pale limestone, revealing the surrounding earth's structure and layers of evolution.

Airplane charters fly daily to the Grand Canyon from Vegas

Rim, accessible by Interstate 40 through the state of Arizona, is the most visited area of the park; the North Rim – arrived at by Interstate 15 through St George, Utah – receives a fraction of that traffic because of the longer journey times. The stunning natural wonder makes an ideal excursion far away from Sin City's glitz. Driving there is the preferable option, for having a car gives access to outstanding scenic overlooks; also access to good walking trails, although, as one visitors' guide says, they are 'narrow and close to the edge,' so agility is desirable. For anyone in a hurry, though, it's possible to take an organized airplane charter trip and return to Vegas the same day.

Rafting and Mule Tours

For active travelers, the park offers backpacking, rafting, and mule-back descents into the canyon. Back-country hiking requires an advance permit; hikes down to the river generally take two days or more, and returning even longer. For more

Trekking in the Grand Canyon by mule train

sedentary visitors, there are historic sites to visit, star-gazing, bird-watching, and, of course, enough spectacular scenery to keep all eyes constantly busy. To travel down into the canyon, plan ahead, and make all your arrangements well in advance.

As for weather, both rims receive snow in the winter, and even summer evenings may be chilly. Due to climate conditions, the North Rim is open only May to October. Down in the canyon, more desert-like conditions prevail, with summer afternoons approaching 120°F (49°C). For more information, tel: 520-638 7864, or call the Las Vegas Convention and Visitors Authority, tel: 702-892 0711.

Zion and Bryce Canyon National Parks

Northeast, in Utah, are the spectacular Zion and Bryce Canyon national parks. Around 155 miles (248km) from Las Vegas, Zion offers natural wonders such as stark rock formations, sheer cliff faces, and rippling waterfalls. The park, accessible year-round, offers hiking trails and scenic drives.

Further north – 210 miles (336km) from Las Vegas – is Bryce Canyon, an amazing series of natural amphitheaters scooped from the edge of the Paunsagunt Plateau by the Paria River. Bryce is known for its colorful formations of sculptured rock – pinnacles, pedestals, fins, and spires.

Sinking Ship, Thor's Hammer, and Natural Bridge, an awesome arch of rock, are just a sample of the canyon's spectacular geological sights.

Great Basin National Park

A five-hour drive from Vegas ends in Great Basin National Park, located along the Nevada-Utah state line. It is well worth the trip to the 77,000 acres (31,160 hectares) of rugged back country, with its groves of ancient bristlecone pine trees and the Lehman Caves, the premier limestone cavern system in the western USA. Head north by using interstates 93 and 50, and state highways 487 and 488.

Death Valley

Death Valley, presumed to be the last resting place of many a gold and silver prospector – actually, only one is known to have died – is 145 miles (232km) west of Las Vegas. Take US95 northwest or Interstate 15 south to Baker, California to get there. Death Valley's many popular destinations include Furnace Creek (which, with a gas station, hotels, and a golf course, is the only dot of civilization), the Devil's Golf Course, Zabriskie Point – immortalized in an arthouse movie of the same name – and the improbable Spanish-Mediteranean Scotty's Castle, completed in 1931 and which, at one time required the labor of 2,000 workmen. The Death Valley National Park Visitors Center can provide maps and information.

Sand dunes in Death Valley

SOUVENIRS
GIFTS
SHIRTS
GLITTER GULCH

WHAT TO DO

Whatever your taste in entertainment and recreation, Las Vegas has something to divert and delight you. From circuses to cocktail bars, from roller coasters to rock and roll, comedy to clubbing, the list is truly endless and the standards are stellar. Gambling may be the main event here, but the sideshows are spectacular.

Cirque du Soleil has set a trend by having an auditorium built around its show, and Vegas resident Celine Dion is following the lead. Due to open in 2003, the Colliseum theater at Ceasars Palace is designed to stage her act.

People-watching is great free entertainment in Las Vegas. Many locals favor the benches by GameWorks to do it.

Until recently, the entertainment in Las Vegas was seen by the casinos as just an adjunct to the gaming. In fact, when Elvis started his 1969 residency at The International (now the Las Vegas Hilton), it was reportedly the first time that a casino made a profit in the showroom.

Now, Las Vegas reaps the rewards and suffers the losses of a metropolis of over one million residents whose primary industry is tourism. This makes the traditional travelers' definitions of 'what to do' and 'where to go' difficult to delineate. In this town, the two overlap. Casinos, resorts, gambling, and entertainment: where does one stop and the next begin? In Sin City they are interrelated, interconnected, and interdependent.

With the overwhelming population explosion that started in the late 1980s came a demand from the locals for more traditional, off-Strip experiences, as a result sparking a growth in culture, sports, and amenities. That process is still young but steadily evolving. Locals and visitors are each feeling their way along a new path for experiencing Las Vegas, one that combines the expected attractions of the gaming and tourism industry with those types of independent cultural and sports amenities found in a more traditional city. The pleasurable result is a combination of the expected and the unexpected.

Gambling

Since 1931, when gambling was officially legalized in Nevada after 22 years of prohibition, it has been used to promote the city. Without question, the primary allure of Las Vegas – despite the resorts, restaurants, showrooms, and shopping malls – is the fact that you can legally place bets on games of chance and sporting events. Make no mistake: the times may be changing, but without gambling, there would be no Forum Shops, no pirate ships, no Guggenheim museums of art.

Most of the gambling in Las Vegas is concentrated along the Strip, where nearly 20 major casinos in excess of 100,000 sq ft (9,300 sq m) beckon passers-by to lighten their pockets a little or a lot and take the chance that they may be among the few who will win the 'Big One.'

At most gaming tables along the Strip, action is fast and furious, with generally inflexible house rules. Downtown casinos are a bit more flexible when it comes to house rules, offering lower minimums and higher (sometimes no) limits. This attracts the unlikely combination of serious career gamblers and novices without much to spend.

Still, the atmosphere is generally more relaxed and amiable, probably due to the fact that Downtown is a concentrated area similar to a

The Riviera

The dealer's invitation

small town – one that has not changed much in 70 years. Still, before you venture into any live gaming area, it is important to familiarize yourself with the rules of the game.

Despite the exceptions mentioned above, most experienced gamblers have little patience for the novice, as they see them as a bad omen in the already frustrating situation of having to beat odds that are set against them. Also, there are strict rules regarding what the player should do with their cards and chips, and where they can place their hands. Disobeying these rules can cost you a bet on the low end; repeated violations can lead to expulsion from the casino.

Card Schools

If you are completely inexperienced, there are several ways to overcome your lack of knowledge. The first is to read about the games. Below is a very brief guide to the most popular games, while books are available to explain the

Dice are made to an accuracy of 1 10,000th of an inch

more complex rules. Another method is to practice on the video versions of these games before moving to live table action. With minimum wagers as low as 5¢ and no other players waiting impatiently for you to make your next move, electronic gaming is an alternative that many novice gamblers never move beyond. Most casinos offer a variety of video game slot machines. Try Bally's casino for the latest selection; after all, they do manufacture most of them.

Despite the potentially intimidating aspects of live gaming, it makes little sense to spend your vacation in Las Vegas and not play at least a few hands of blackjack or craps, especially when there are free gaming lessons offered at several different casinos. Dealers teach groups who have more-or-less equal ability, so no one feels pressured or out of place. This hands-on method is the best way to learn a game and its rules without risking your money or your pride.

Baccarat

Typically assumed to be a high-roller card game, baccarat *(bah-cah-rah)* is similar to blackjack, though it's played with stricter rules, higher limits, and less player interaction. The object of the game is to come as close as possible to 9; the only real skill involved is deciding whether to bet on the player or the bank (i.e., the dealer). Most baccarat tables are located in quiet, sequestered sections of the casino. Gambling lessons are highly recommended for this game.

Big 6 (or Money Wheel)

This spin-and-win game resembles a prize game offered in the carnivals of old. The game is easy – simply bet on one of the numbers – which makes it attractive to novices, but the house edge makes them leave equally quickly, and usually poorer.

Bingo

Nearly everyone knows the game of bingo, the mini-lottery in which players try to line up a horizontal or a vertical row of randomly drawn numbers. The numbers are called out until someone wins; a few veterans get up to 10 cards playing at once. No lessons required.

Black Jack (or 21)

This is the most popular live table game gamblers play in Las Vegas – and the easiest card game to learn – owing to its

Hoping to win a fortune

relative simplicity. The object is to play against the dealer (house) and draw cards as close to 21 as possible without 'busting' (going over 21). There are several optional bets – splitting, doubling down, insurance (never take insurance) – and variations that include single-deck vs. multi-deck card shoes, and hands dealt face-up (as opposed to one card down). The house advantage is that if you bust, the dealer takes your money even if he busts as well.

Craps

This is the raucous game of cheering (and cursing) crowds, where everyone at the table has a stake in what one hapless gambler does with the dice. Loud players, dramatically placed chips, and flying dice all revolve around a set of complex betting rules, and the fact that 7 is more likely to be rolled than any other number. Bets are placed both for and

Odds can be high at roulette

against the dice thrower (or 'shooter'). Money changes hands very quickly at a craps table, making it another good candidate for lessons, and it's not as complicated as it looks. But don't even lean against a craps table unless you know what you're doing, or have plenty of money to lose.

Many casinos issue special chips for events like New Year, and players often prefer to collect them than cash them in.

Keno

Another game similar to a lottery, keno is usually played sitting in a casino coffee shop. Unlike bingo, however, the odds are shifted in that players circle random numbers on a purchased ticket and wait for a fixed set of numbers to be drawn. It's easy to play: pick up to 15 numbers on the 80-number slip, then hand it and your money (usually $1 per game) to the keno runner, and she'll return a computerized ticket. Watch the illuminated keno board above to see if enough of your numbers come up to win. The odds of winning are very low – in fact, the house advantage is greater than that of any other casino game – but it's an inexpensive way to pass the time while you're eating.

Poker

A high-stakes card game played in a high-pressure atmosphere. Unlike most other card games, gamblers here play against each other; the house operates the game for a fixed percentage of each pot, usually 5 percent. There are many variations on offer, from the standard 7-card stud to Texas Hold 'Em. If you're new to the game, this might be an expensive place to learn. If you are a poker regular, Las Vegas is a great place to play, but watch out. As the old poker adage goes, 'Sit at the table, and figure out who the fool is. If you still don't know after five minutes, get up and leave. It's bound to be you.'

Pai Gow

If you enjoy poker, gambling at a mild pace, and playing against no house advantage, you'll love Pai Gow. Each player is dealt seven cards, which are then arranged by the player into two piles: one five-card hand and one two-card hand. Standard poker rules apply; that is, pairs, straights, flushes, full houses, are ranked in a hierarchy of hands to determine the winner. The five-card hand must beat the two-card hand, and both hands must beat the dealer's two hands in order to win. If only one of the dealer's hands wins, the game is a 'push' (tie), and no money changes hands (this happens more often than not). If both the dealer's hands win, you lose. It's perfectly acceptable to ask the dealer for advice on how to play your hand (and a great way to learn). The caveat is that since the house has no advantage, it takes 5 percent of your winnings.

Slot machines are the most popular game in Vegas

Roulette

Another subdued game of European flair, roulette does not enjoy much popularity in Las Vegas. It's a relatively simple game, where bets are placed by laying chips on a single number or groups of numbers, colors, or even/odd. Different players are given different colored chips to avoid confusion. The wheel is spun, the ball drops, and where it lands determines the outcome. Odds are as high as 35 to 1, which means a single $5 chip on the right number wins you $175. (Handy hint: avoid playing a double-zero wheel and search for those with only one zero.) Winning numbers are illuminated at each table to attract passers-by into thinking 'It's hitting my number!'

Siegfried & Roy's tigers gambol at the Mirage

Slot Machines

Slot machines have become the most popular form of gaming in Las Vegas – so much so that they supersede the play at table games in many casinos. Though all modern slot machines are computerized, the rules are the same: get three or four matching icons in a row (or some combination thereof) and you win. The difference is that the computer decides when you win, not pure chance. And even though the payback increases the more you bet on a single pull, the computer will decrease your odds of winning. The skill, they say, is to find a slot machine that's 'hitting'; that is, a computer that's programmed to pay out big money. Ask the coin collectors which are the 'loosest slots.' Remember, if you win, they'll expect a tip.

Video Poker

Video poker has become increasingly popular, so much so that there's hardly a bar, grocery store, or laundromat in Las Vegas that doesn't have at least two or three machines. It's the same as regular five-card stud, with the machine acting as dealer. Unlike slots, interaction and a semblance of skill are required; that is, you are offered a choice on how to play the hand you're dealt. A chart on the screen lists the payoff of your winning hand and, as with slots, the more you bet, the better the payoff. Versions of video poker range from 'Jacks or Better' (the standard game) to 'Double Bonus' or 'Deuces Wild,' although the more wild cards involved, the lower the payoff.

THE BIG SHOWS

Once, Las Vegas showrooms were filled with top-notch entertainment – headliners, comedians, production shows, and dancing girls – all at a very low price. In that bygone era, elaborate dinner shows were seen by the casinos as a loss leader, a way to keep customers happily dropping money at the tables or the slot machines. As long as the bottom line was glittering, the casino operators, especially during the days of the Mob, were happy to continue providing entertainment and food very inexpensively, or even for free.

Weddings

Getting married almost ranks as a sport in Las Vegas, America's favorite city in which to tie the knot. More than 100,000 couples take the plunge here every year. Dozens of celebrities, including Michael Jordan, Elvis Presley, Paul Newman, and Richard Gere, have exchanged vows in Vegas; many of the chapels on Las Vegas Boulevard and Main Street have signs boasting of the big names they've joined in matrimony. Most weddings are anything but traditional. You can have an Elvis impersonator sing your nuptials at the Graceland Wedding Chapel (tel: 702-474 6655), use the drive-up wedding window at Chapel by the Courthouse (tel: 702-384 9099), or, if you're up to it, get married in a helicopter over the Strip. Other options range from a bungee-jumping ceremony to saying your vows on a boat on Lake Mead. Theme weddings – with everyone dressed in 'Star Trek' suits or medieval costume, for instance – have also become popular.

When corporations moved in with more stringent departmental accounting procedures, every sector of a hotel-casino had to show success. Not satisfied with a simple overall profit, corporate operators began to both raise prices and cut corners, resulting in an era of frustrating mediocrity from which Las Vegas has only recently emerged.

Every year, more than 100,000 couples get married in Las Vegas

Now, most showrooms are again offering quality stars and elaborate productions, *sans* the accompanying dinner service. Prices have certainly risen, but so has the benchmark of quality. Some of the bigger shows and headliner appearances (especially during major events like New Year's Eve) exceed over $100 per ticket – typical for New York, but previously unheard of in Las Vegas. What this means is that, in the case of showroom entertainers, the old adage of 'getting what you pay for' now applies to Las Vegas.

Keeping up with the Shows

Although the runs for the shows listed here are considered open-ended, remember that nothing is static in Las Vegas. Entire resorts open and close, and showrooms sometimes change show times, prices, or featured productions. Also, there are numerous headlining entertainers who change from week to week. For current listings of all the resort entertainment, pick up a free copy of *Showbiz Weekly* or *What's On In Las Vegas,* the two most comprehensive listings guides. In the reviews below, 'dark' refers to the day when the show does not play at all. Be advised that it is an old tradition for showgirls in Las Vegas production shows to be topless, and that tradition continues; so many of the shows are not appropriate for children.

American Superstars: Of the cavalcade of impersonator shows, this one is skewed heavily toward the modern era. Talented performers provide energetic renditions of Madonna, Michael Jackson, Ricky Martin, and Christina Aguilera, among others. The *Las Vegas Advisor* recently said this show was the 'best value in town.' *Stratosphere Hotel and Casino, 2000 Las Vegas Boulevard South; tel: 702-380 7777. Shows 7 and 10pm, no late show Sunday–Tuesday; dark Thursday; (special rate for children 4–12 years of age).*

Blue Man Group: This award-winning show features three bald, blue characters. The one-of-a-kind showroom experience has been called innovative, hilarious, and musically powerful. *Luxor Hotel and Casino, 3900 Las Vegas Boulevard South; tel: 702-262 4100. Shows 7 and 10pm (no late show Sunday and Monday); dark Tuesday.*

Lance Burton – Master Magician: Set in one of the most magnificent environments in Las Vegas – an impeccably gilded theater that somehow maintains intimacy – magician Lance Burton pulls off extraordinary illusions with the assistance of a talented group of dancers. *Monte Carlo Hotel and Casino, 3770 Las Vegas Boulevard South; tel: 702-730 7777. Shows 7 and 10pm; dark Sunday and Monday.*

Caesars Magical Empire: A particularly unusual interactive dinner and show experience set in a series of elaborately themed underground chambers rather than a showroom proper. Entertainers and illusionists perform for diners, who move to another chamber for more illusions. Fun for both adults and children. *Caesars Palace Hotel and Casino, 3570 Las Vegas Boulevard South; tel: 702-731 7110. Multiple seatings from 5pm; dark Sunday and Monday (special rate for children 5–10 years of age).*

***Cirque du Soleil's* Mystère**: The internationally famed Cirque takes the circus to new levels of sophistication in an amazing state-of-the-art theater. No animals are used in this circus, just 72 performers of amazing physical and emotive skill and grace. A unique Las Vegas experience that borders on performance art. This popular show spawned the aquatic show at the Bellagio. *Treasure Island, 3300 Las Vegas Boulevard South; tel: 702-894 7111. Shows 7:30 and 10:30pm; dark Monday and Tuesday.*

***Cirque du Soleil's* O**: From the acclaimed international troupe, *O* dazzles in an aquatic environment that utilizes 1½ million gallons (6.8 million liters) of water. Around 75

The Folies Bergères

***Mystére*, the Cirque du Soleil show at Treasure Island**

skilled performers perform on a remarkable stage. *Bellagio Hotel and Casino, 3600 Las Vegas Boulevard South; tel: 702-693 7111. Shows 7:30 and 11pm; dark Wednesday and Thursday.*

Celine Dion has signed a $45 million three-year engagement to perform at least five shows a week in a purpose-built showroom at Caesars Palace. The 4,000 seat Colliseum is due to open in the spring of 2003. *Caesars Palace, 3570 Las Vegas Boulevard South, tel: 702 731-7110.*

EFX: A grand $45 million production show in a classic but updated style. Featuring a host of original music sung by the main star and dozens of other singing and dancing talents, EFX is a special-effects laden science-fiction tale suitable for all ages. *MGM Grand Hotel and Casino, 3799 Las Vegas Boulevard South; tel: 702-891 7777. Shows 7:30 and 10:30pm; dark Sunday and Monday.*

Folies Bergères: The Las Vegas home of the famous topless dancers since 1961, the Tropicana's show was recently revamped and updated. Nothing says 'Las Vegas' quite like this; the glittering costumes and chorus line of showgirls is what the myth is based on. *Tropicana Resort and Casino, 3801 Las Vegas Boulevard South; tel: 702-739 2222. Shows 7:30 and 10pm; dark Thursday.*

Danny Gans – The Man of Many Voices: What started as a short-lived Las Vegas stint at the Stratosphere Tower has evolved into one of the most popular shows in town. Gans is an amazing impersonator and an energetic showman who has mastered the art of entertainment. *Mirage Hotel and Casino, 7900 Las Vegas Boulevard South; tel: 702-791 7111. Shows 8pm; dark Monday and Friday.*

Jubilee!: Long before the blockbuster movie, *Jubilee!* was sinking the *Titanic* on the Strip in what is the show's signature amazing special effect. The show also features magician Dirk Arthur and dozens of topless and costumed showgirls, making this an event for adults only. *Bally's Hotel and Casino, 3645 Las Vegas Boulevard South; tel: 702-739 4111. Shows 7:30 and 10:30pm Wednesday to Monday; dark Tuesday.*

King Arthur's Tournament: A radical departure from modern Las Vegas stage shows, this one features two unusual elements: live horses and dinner – the latter of which is eaten without utensils. A re-creation of a medieval knights' jousting tournament, it's great fun for families. *Excalibur Hotel and Casino, 3850 Las Vegas Boulevard South; tel: 702-597 7777. Shows 6 and 8:30pm.*

Legends In Concert: A strong favorite of many return visitors, this classic Las Vegas impersonation show features all the greats from yesterday and today. Impersonators render uncanny performances of the Four Tops and Elvis, as well as modern stars like Garth Brooks and Shania Twain. *Imperial Palace Hotel and Casino, 3535 Las Vegas Boulevard South; tel: 702-731 3311. Shows 7:30 and 10:30pm; dark Sunday.*

Wayne Newton: Las Vegas' consummate entertainer, Wayne Newton croons to audiences six nights a week in an elaborate theater named for 'Mr Vegas' himself. *Stardust Resort and Casino, 3000 Las Vegas Boulevard South; tel:*

The fabulous Desert Passage

702-732 6111. Shows 9pm Sunday to Thursday; 8 and 11pm Saturday; dark Friday.

Siegfried & Roy: These world-famous illusionists and Las Vegas residents have risen from a small-time specialty act to stardom. Their famous white tigers are an integral part of the spectacular show, set in a 1,500-seat showroom. *Mirage Hotel and Casino, 3400 Las Vegas Boulevard South; tel: 702-791 7444. Shows 7:30 and 11pm; dark Wednesday and Thursday.*

Splash: One of the few remaining 'traditional' Vegas production shows, *Splash* features a large cast of singers and dancers who perform around variety acts. There are numerous set and theme changes, plenty of water use, and a number in which the dancers (performing topless at the late show) come out into the audience. *Riviera Hotel and Casino, 2901 Las Vegas Boulevard South; tel: 702-734 5110. Shows 7:30 and 10:30pm.*

SHOPPING

Where there is money, there is shopping, and shopping facilities have always been around in Vegas. But compared with other major cities, these facilities didn't live up to expectation. Hotel shopping areas consisted of retailers selling mostly expensive and tacky (or sometimes cheap and tacky) merchandise, and malls were nothing more than utilitarian outlets. In recent years, this scenario has changed dramatically.

As the city expands, so do the shopping facilities. Groups of stores are now marketed as 'retail destinations' and compete with the casinos in sound, light, and entertainment amenities. The Forum Shops (at Caesars Palace) started the trend, placing its outlets under an indoor 'sky' that changes color, simulating dawn to dusk several times a day. Desert Passage took this a step further: as well as an indoor 'rainstorm', the facades of its stores are beautifully landscaped, echoing the Arabian theme of its neighbor casino, the Aladdin. Elegant hotel-based shopping promenades have also emerged at the Venetian and Bellagio resorts. The Fashion Show Mall, long resident on the Strip, entered 2003 with a bang, increasing its floor space underneath a gigantic outdoor 'cloud'.

There are also several outlet malls within a short drive, and a few local stores that merit a visit.

Shopping Malls

The **Forum Shops**, located at Caesars Palace casino, was the first themed indoor shopping promenade, built

The Fashion Show Mall now has more stores than ever

to look and feel like an outdoor Roman street. It surprised quite a few observers in 1992 by attracting not only the obvious tourists from the Strip, but also more than a handful of shopping-starved locals eager to explore stores they once had to travel out-of-state to visit. The number of restaurants and entertainment outlets made the Forum a great place for an all-day, one-stop spending spree, and fueled the trend for others; great fun for the whole family is the opulent **Desert Passage** at the Aladdin.

Not to be left behind, resort-casinos decided their guests (and a novelty-seeking public) would enjoy having retail possibilities that matched the caliber of their hotels. As expected, upscale stores like Tiffany, Versace, and Prada dominate **Shopping le Boulevard** at Paris Las Vegas and **Via Bellagio** at Bellagio, while the **Grand Canal Shoppes** is a major part of the Venetian's centerpiece attraction.

Belz Factory Outlet for bargains

The Fashion Show Mall is the largest shopping destination on the Strip, attracting good key stores like Saks, Lord & Taylor, Macy's, and Nordstrom. In late 2003, it is kicking out all the stops with a massive start-of-the-art Great Hall that will be used for fashion shows and product-launch events (including cars), and a signature architectural steel 'cloud' canopy rising 20 stories into the air and employed as a huge projection canvas during the evening.

The Galleria at Sunset is a recent suburban shopping mall, located in the upscale Green Valley area in the nearby town of Henderson. Across from the Sunset Station Hotel and Casino, the mall houses a selection of interesting specialty stores in addition to department stores and a massive food court.

Factory Outlet Malls

The **Fashion Outlets of Las Vegas** at Primm, Nevada (on the California state line) is an important entry into the outlet mall roster, and the best by far. Though it requires a 30-minute drive from the Tropicana via Interstate 15 (or a several-time-daily shuttle bus from New York-New York; tel: 1-888-424 6898), the Fashion Outlet's selection of top names (Versace, Kenneth Cole, Tommy Hilfiger) and specialty stores make it worth the effort.

Within Las Vegas Valley and not far away from the Strip (although you may need a car) is the **Belz Factory Outlet World**. Belz, an indoor mall, offers 145 outlet stores with bargain opportunities ranging from clothing to electronics.

Local Shopping

Beyond the malls lie hundreds of unique specialty stores. From ethnic food and vintage clothing stores to electronics and book stores, there are many interesting shopping spots that escape the attention of most tourists. Here are a few

Walking the malls can be hard on the feet, just like the miles of casino aisles. For comfort, wear soft-soled shoes.

highlights; for the names of more specialty stores, pick up one of the free newsweeklies, *CityLife* or *Las Vegas Weekly.*

The Attic, tel: 702-388 4088, may be the most famous vintage store in America, owing to it featuring in both a Visa credit-card commercial and on extreme sports TV network ESPN II. This two-story collection of clothes, appliances, and knick-knacks serves a willing audience with its selection of period clothing, often being called upon to provide items for movies being filmed in Las Vegas.

At the other end of the retail scale, the **Tower/Good Guys/WOW! Multimedia Superstore**, tel: 702-364 2500, sells nothing even remotely vintage, except perhaps within its vast CD selection. A combined effort of Tower Records and the Good Guys Electronics, WOW! overwhelms in every way. There's a huge electronics and computer selection featuring a home theater room and a classical listening room, plus innumerable aisles of records, books, software, CDs, and the city's largest selection of periodicals and magazines. At the fulcrum is a coffee bar and café under a giant-screen TV flanked by CD listening stations.

Anyone who wears glasses will appreciate the Strip location of **Optica of Las Vegas**, tel: 702-735 8557, a full service optometry store that repairs eyewear, provides exams, and sets visitors up with a new set of prescription glasses or contact lenses – all within a couple of days. The designer-frame selection is among the best in town.

For souvenirs of the innately Las Vegas kind, there is the **Gamblers' General Store**, tel: 702-382 9903, a centrally located supplier of slot machines, gaming tables, and other gaming accoutrements. Most items can be shipped for the purchaser if requested.

For a taste of authentic Native American tobacco, the **Paiute Tribal Smoke Shop**, tel: 702-387 6433 sells tax-free tobacco products through its drive-through window, so you can cruise right back to the hotel, light up, and spend all that money you just saved.

SPORTS

Las Vegas is a sporting city. Whether you want to watch championship boxing matches, bet on the New York Giants at a Sports Book, go para-gliding, skiing, or play 18 holes of golf, all it takes is the right toys and/or plenty of cash. If you engage in any outdoor sport, though, remember that valley temperatures can reach well above 100°F (38°C) in summer and below freezing in winter, so it's very important to follow any local precautions, like using sunscreen or buying thermal underwear.

Nevada's hills are perfect for mountain biking

The Las Vegas Motor Speedway

Spectator Sports

Boxing

Las Vegas has a long boxing history, having hosted enough championship fights to qualify as a capital of the sport. A big-time bout at one of the three resorts that handles most of the action – the MGM Grand, Caesars Palace, or the Mirage – invariably draws a crowd heavy on celebrities.

Bowling

Las Vegas has always had an affinity for bowling. The PBA holds both national and senior televized tournaments here at the Showboat Bowling Center in January.

Golf Tournaments

The Las Vegas Invitational held every fall – known as the first professional tournament for famed champion Tiger Woods in 1996 – is considered the city's top golf attraction.

Three courses split the action: the Southern Highlands, the TPC at the Canyons, and the main course, the TPC at Summerlin. The TPC at the Canyons is also home to the Las Vegas Senior Classic, a draw for golf's big names held every spring. Check out the PGA website at <www.pgatour.com> for up-to-date information about tournaments, and for other local golfing events.

Motor Sports

Serious auto racing arrived in Las Vegas in 1996 with the opening of the Las Vegas Motor Speedway, 17 miles (27km) north of Downtown on Interstate 15. The 1,500-acre (607-hectare) site is a speed-freak's dream: a 1½-mile (2.5-km) tri-oval super speedway, plus smaller clay and paved ovals, a drag strip, a road track, and a motocross course. Race fans fill the 107,000-seat facility for NASCAR events like the Las Vegas 300, Winston West, and Craftsman Truck races, as well as the IRL Las Vegas 500.

The National Finals Rodeo

Held every December, this is one of the largest rodeo events in the country. It's an action-packed 10-day festival of the nation's top cowboys and cowgirls riding bulls, busting broncos, and roping calves at the Thomas and Mack Center. The city goes Western with endless satellite events, like beauty pageants, parties and dances at bars, cowboy-themed art exhibits, musical events at Downtown's Fremont Street Experience, and golf tournaments. If you want to attend, be sure to plan well ahead, as last-minute tickets for the big rodeo events are hard to come by.

Other Sports

While lacking a major sports franchise, Las Vegas is home to a triple-A baseball team and a Minor-League hockey squad.

The Las Vegas Stars – the city's longest-running professional sports outfit – is a farm team for baseball's San Diego Padres; tickets are usually available for the Cashman Field home games. The Las Vegas Thunder hockey team (which is not affiliated with any NHL franchise) competes in the Thomas and Mack Center. During football and basketball seasons, the University of Nevada-Las Vegas fields teams in both sports. UNLV's basketball team has a storied history, winning the NCAA title in 1990.

Participatory Sports

Bicycling

Avoid putting your mettle to the peddle on Sin City's busier streets; bicycle paths are few and courteous drivers even fewer. The best places are local parks or cycle-friendly spots beyond Vegas' city limits. One favorite: the 13-mile (21-km) scenic loop at Red Rock Canyon *(see page 64)*, takes cyclists through some of the area's more picturesque landscapes and is not overly taxing.

Mountain bikers can call Escape the City Streets, tel: 702-596 2953, to arrange a more rugged ride through the canyon's Cottonwood Valley. Another good bet: Floyd Lamb State Park, a few miles north on US95. These bike paths wind among ponds, trees, and historic buildings.

Golf

For a desert city, Las Vegas has more than enough grass fairways and water hazards to keep the most avid duffer busy. For a locator map and a course-by-course description, go to <www.lasvegasfreedom.com>. The Rio All-Suites Hotel maintains a course several miles away from the Strip for the use of their guests that offers spectacular views of the Las Vegas Valley. Angel Park Golf Club, tel: 702-254 4653 is a municipal course with a difference: it has two 18-hole courses designed by Arnold Palmer and a 12-hole par-3 course featuring replicas of famous par-3 holes from around the world.

The Las Vegas Paiute Resort, tel: 702-658 1400 is 20 miles (32km) north of town but well worth the trip: one of its two courses – called Snow Mountain – was designated the best public course in Southern Nevada by *Golf Digest*. Also beyond city limits is the Legacy Golf Club, tel: 702-897 2200 in the nearby suburb of Henderson.

Hiking

The Las Vegas Valley is rimmed with quality hiking trails. One of the more scenic is the 5-mile (8-km) River Mountain Trail with fine views of Lake Mead and the valley. Red Rock Canyon affords numerous routes, including a 2-mile (3-km) Pine Creek Canyon trek and a slightly longer walk along the Keystone Thrust Trail. Mount Charleston is webbed with good hikes; the ranger station can supply information, tel: 702-873 8800. Another fine spot is the Valley of Fire *(see page 64)*.

The Vegas area has many good golf courses

Rock Climbing

Red Rock Canyon, just 20 minutes from the Strip, has

Bally's showgirls

the best rock climbing in the region. There are literally thousands of climbing challenges, from small bouldering routes to towering, experts-only cliffs. Spring and fall are optimum climbing seasons, but on almost any weekend there will be a cross-section of the international rock-jock community roping up in the canyon. Sky's the Limit guide service, tel: 702-363 4533 can arrange climbing trips of nearly any duration.

Snow Sports

Mount Charleston has a ski area, the Las Vegas Ski and Snowboard Resort, also known as Lee Canyon, tel: 702-872 5462. It has bunny, intermediate, and expert routes, along with all the trappings: ski rental, ski school, and a lounge. The natural snowfall is often augmented by snow-making equipment to ensure adequate powder. The resort has nine long runs on 40 acres (16 hectares), but despite its name, snowboarding is allowed only at certain times.

Tennis

Most resorts have tennis facilities, but these are often for guests only. Otherwise, the Las Vegas Sporting House, tel: 702-733 8999, a membership sporting club, makes its courts available to nonmembers as well. Additional courts open to the public can be found in the city's Lorenzi Park.

ADULT ENTERTAINMENT

For all the hype about Las Vegas's conversion to a family town, the truth is that beyond all the shiny big-name properties lies a bevy of adult-oriented distractions. While in recent years efforts have been made to eliminate many of these attractions, the fact is that most of the seedier or disreputable businesses have disappeared, while those operating within the law have actually flourished. As a result, Las Vegas seems ready to accept the multiple layers of complexity its status as a tourist city throws up.

Many of the resorts on the Strip have appeased family visitors by cleaning up their shows and covering up their showgirls. But at the **Riviera** all four shows are adult-oriented (though *Splash* is covered for the early show); for raucous fun, choose *Crazy Girls* – a review that gets even more outrageous

Casinos and Kids

By law, people under the age of 21 are not permitted in any casino gaming areas, bars, or lounges, but some casinos are child-friendly if certain rules are followed (children must not be left unattended; children may walk through a casino when accompanied by a parent but may not stop). Other casinos ban strollers from the premises or close the doors entirely to anyone under 18 unless they are guests staying with an adult. If you are a parent desperate for a little grown-up fun, however, most hotels can arrange babysitting services.

during convention season. There's also the long-running *Folies Bergères*, now an institution and not to be missed. But its early-evening shows, too, have been toned down.

There are dozens of clubs other than casinos that offer either nude or topless entertainment. Of the topless-only clubs (all of which have full bars), the two best are **Cheetah's Topless Lounge**, 2112 Western Avenue, an intimate, friendly place, and **Olympic Garden Cabaret**, 1531 Las Vegas Boulevard South, which, with 11 full-size stages, is just the opposite. For totally nude dancers, the choices are just as varied, but only one – the **Palomino Club**, 1848 Las Vegas Boulevard North – serves alcohol, due to Vegas' complicated licensing laws. Of the clubs that are 'dry,' the best bet is the tastefully decorated but oddly named **Spearmint Rhino**, 3340 South Highland Drive.

NIGHTLIFE

From local bars featuring live music and comedy to nightclubs, cafes, and coffeehouses, the city's after-dusk life beyond gambling and shows is very healthy. For a detailed listing of local events beyond the Strip, pick up one of the two free alternative newsweeklies, *CityLife* or *Las Vegas Weekly.*

After the heady days of the 1950s, nightclubbing took a nose-dive but is now extremely popular again, thanks to a resurgence of dance music and the city's population boom. **Club Utopia** on the Strip (but not in a hotel) may be single-handedly responsible for reviving the scene by taking the metropolitan sounds of techno and house out of the underground and into a commercial venue for the first time. That, along with the success of **Club Rio** in the Rio All-Suites Hotel, led to a deluge of hotel-based high-energy clubs, including **Ra** in the Luxor, **Studio 54** in the MGM Grand and more opening every season. Each club caters to a specific crowd, so hunt around until you find the right one.

The Strip at its best; at night

Drinking and Dancing

Some nightclubs place as much emphasis on drinking as dancing, including **Drink Las Vegas**, a fabulous two-story club with numerous bars serving every drink known to man or bartender. **The Beach** is also two stories tall, with waiters and waitresses dressed for sunbathing – they often jump on the bar for a little bikini dancing.

Lesbian and gay travelers can discover integrated nightlife in the so-called 'Gay Triangle' area on Paradise Road. **Gipsy** is small but packed wall-to-wall with energetic dancing (it's mostly men here, though women are welcome). Across the street, **Lace** is a tiny women's disco located in the back of Angles video bar.

Cafe Society

The local cafe scene is surprisingly strong for a city with so many Starbucks outlets. **Cafe Copioh** is a well-known haunt

The scary Big Shot

of university students and professors, and hosts a calendar of events ranging from poetry readings to live music. Nearby is the venerable **Cafe Espresso Roma** – the oldest coffeehouse in Las Vegas and, according to many regulars, still the best in all its Bohemian glory.

For less caffeine and more food, across town in the Downtown Gateway District is the egalitarian **Enigma Garden Cafe**. Lawyers, poets, city councilmen, and starving musicians take advantage day and night of its garden setting and large menu featuring items with names of historic Las Vegas importance. In the opposite direction you might enjoy **Jazzed Cafe and Vinotec**, a charming bistro with an extensive by-the-glass wine list and a carefully crafted menu of Tuscan specialties, accompanied by acid jazz, *tiramisù* and espresso. Best of all, the doors stay open until about 4am.

LAS VEGAS FOR CHILDREN

Although Las Vegas is now an adult town again, there are a surprising number of kid-friendly activities. Most casinos have at least some kind of arcade, but the true high-scorer is **GameWorks** next to the MGM Grand, with 47,000 sq ft (4,371 sq m) of games (more than 250) from traditional pinball outposts to high-tech diversions. If you play up an appetite, GameWorks also has a full-service restaurant, snack bar, and Starbucks Coffee outlet. Adults can relax in the bar and shoot pool while the kiddies shoot the arcade games.

Races, Rides, and Virtual Reality

Add a little zoom to your kids' day with a stop at **Sahara Speedworld**, a huge (40,000-sq-ft /3,720-sq-m) playground of virtual reality auto racing in life-size race cars, dozens of interactive rides, and two 3-D theaters.

Visitors between May and September can take tots and teens alike for a cool dip at the **Wet 'N Wild** water park – complete with kiddie pools and knee-buckling water slides. Der Stuka offers a seven-story drop, while the Black Hole shoots you through a dark tunnel. Or just float along in the slow-moving lazy river or drift in a large wave pool.

Decades ago, Circus Circus inaugurated the era of family friendly hotel-casinos, and in recent years has tried to up the ante with **Adventuredome**, a pink-dome-covered, climate-controlled cluster of attractions: the Canyon Blaster corkscrew roller coaster, a water ride, bumper cars, carnival games, and a laser tag arena. It's located behind the venerable hotel-casino, which itself features kid-friendly free circus acts from 11am to midnight daily.

Roller-coaster aficionados will want to hop aboard the twisting, turning, looping **Manhattan Express roller coaster** at New York-New York. Once inside the hotel, stop at the extensive Coney Island-themed arcade. Ultra high-altitude thrills are available from atop the Stratosphere Tower. The **Big Shot** slingshot ride heightens the sensation of sudden vertical acceleration with its setting 1,100ft (335m) above the city. The **High Roller roller coaster** is up there too, but experienced riders consider the attraction too slow and uneventful, despite its giddying altitude.

Manhattan Express roller coaster, New York-New York

Next to the MGM Grand and not far from Game-Works is **M&M World**, four stories of merchandise and memorabilia dedicated to the small, round candies. Inside, the miles of aisles are loaded with thousands of M&M-related knickknacks, souvenirs, and collectibles; for sheer novelty, sample the hard-to-find silver M&Ms.

Want to attract the kids away from the Strip and the casinos? Try the three-course miniature golf, bumper boats, go-karts, and arcade games at **Scandia Family Fun Center**, tel: 702-364 0070.

Wild-West Town

Even farther from the lights is **Bonnie Springs-Old Nevada**, tel: 702-875 4191, a mock ghost town near Red Rock Canyon. The Wild-West town comes complete with gunfights, a wax museum, an opera house, a mini-train, horseback riding, and an extensive petting zoo.

For motorized thrills, Las Vegas has at least one grand prix go-cart course. **Las Vegas Mini Grand Prix**, tel: 702-259 7000, has the West's only banked-oval stock car track. Parents, bring your driving gloves – along with go-karts and kiddie karts, the 7-acre (3-hectare) facility provides wheels for big drivers, too.

For something a little more assertive, try **Desert Storm Paintball**, tel: 702-595 2555. Budding warriors – minimum age 10 – are armed with paintball guns, then set loose as all hell breaks out. Wear old clothes.

Calendar of Events

January *The Super Bowl:* The biggest sports-betting day of the year; Sports Books are packed with anxious betters watching the game on giant-screen televisions.

PBA Classic: A major stop on the Pro Bowlers tour, taking place at the Showboat every year.

February *Las Vegas International Marathon:* Really only a half marathon, but who could pass up the opportunity to run from Jean, Nevada, to the Strip on the old LA Highway?

April *World Series of Poker:* 21 tournaments and prize money in the millions make this the biggest draw in the card world, attracting top players and crowds of spectators from all over the globe to Binion's Horseshoe in downtown Las Vegas.

June *Helldorado Days:* A four-day rodeo, plus western parties and pageants celebrate Southern Nevada's cowpoke roots.

September *Las Vegas 500K IRL Race and NASCAR Craftsman Truck Series:* In one of the biggest weekend racing combinations in the US, these two races have been scheduled on the same weekend at the end of September since 1999.

October *PGA Las Vegas Invitational:* this four-day, internationally televised golf tournament from the Tournament Players Club in Summerlin is a major event on the world's golfing calendar.

November *COMDEX:* When the consumer-electronics industry descends on Las Vegas, geek world comes to town, meaning the streets are packed with traffic, hotel rooms are booked, and topless bars are crammed with revelers waving $1 bills.

December *CineVegas:* The premiere four-day film festival in Las Vegas always features a strong showing of unreleased films, festival winners, independents, and classics.

New Year's Eve: Celebrate with 200,000 or more of your newest friends. Las Vegas's celebrations and the two major block parties that accompany them are challenging Times Square for attendees. Make your reservations early and come prepared to party.

EATING OUT

Dining in Las Vegas has been transformed. The wall-to-wall all-you-can-eat buffets have been sidelined, the celebrity chefs are here, and the standards and the stakes (steaks) have been raised all round. Although the high-ticket gastrodomes may not be perfect for every meal, they have definitely raised the culinary game. Prices in these eateries have nearly caught up with their New York, LA and San Franciscan cousins, but so, too, has the food and the service.

Catering at the more down-to-earth kitchens has become more expensive too, but the food is a lot better than the curling buffet fayre of old. Sitting side-by-side with the paying customers are a new breed. Gamblers are regularly rewarded for their play by pit bosses scribbling out 'comps' (complimentary tickets) for the hotel's on-site restaurants. The level of the comp depends upon the level of play, so everyone – low-rollers to big spenders – can be accommodated. And what could be better than a free meal in Las Vegas?

Fanning the flames at a Vegas steak house

Cuisines of the World

With the arrival of Wolfgang Puck's Spago in 1992, the city began a slow but sure ascent from the depths of continental cuisine into the modern world of the nouvelle, haute, California, Pan Asian, and Pacific Rim. Since then, more 'name' chefs have brought their operations to Las Vegas, among them Emeril Lagasse and Jean-Louis Palladin.

Waterside dining at Canaletto, the Venetian

New on the Menu

Acting in concert with these arrivals was the hotels' new-found willingness to relinquish ownership and management of some of their dining spaces to experienced restaurateurs. The result for food lovers has been terrific. The improvement of the dining experience and the resulting rise of expectations led to an across-the-board renewal. Today, some of the city's – and even the country's – best restaurants are ensconced within hotel-casinos, such as Picasso at Bellagio, Postrio at the Venetian, the New Orleans Fish House at the MGM Grand, and Napa at the Rio All-Suites Resort.

Bountiful Buffets

Despite these changes to the culinary landscape, buffets can still be a hit-and-miss affair, with many offering similar selections of prime rib, starchy vegetables, limp salads, and boring desserts. Others offer a wide array of cuisines – Mexican, Italian, American heartland (in other words, meat and potatoes), and vegetables – plus all the seconds, thirds, and fourths you can gulp down. The tantalizing buffets of lore – where the food is imaginatively selected and the prices low – do exist, but it may require searching them out.

The Feast at Palace Station is in this category, as is Main Street Station's Garden Court Buffet. The Rio's Carnival World Buffet is also very good and has an incredibly large selection. But it and the very best (the Golden Nugget's The Buffet) are no longer rock-bottom cheap, and all buffets, regardless of class, status, price, or time of day or night, have lines that stretch around the block.

Champagne Brunch

Sunday champagne brunches were once the best of the buffets, despite champagne that was not always palatable. Today, most are simply a more expensive version of the standard breakfast-lunch offerings. Bally's Sterling Brunch is a notable exception. Replete with ice sculptures, and fresh flowers, it is a spread fit for a king, but it is also the most expensive.

Theme restaurants have proliferated in Las Vegas. Local versions of the Hard Rock Cafe and the Harley Davidson Cafe pull the same surprisingly brisk business that they do around the globe. One of the traditional areas of any major tourist city – a so-called restaurant row – has evolved piece-

Celebrity Chefs

The arrival of celebrity chefs has transformed the Las Vegas dining landscape. Of only 18 North American chefs to win five stars in a recent Mobil Travel guide, two cook at Bellagio restaurants. Tim Zagat, of the Zagat restaurant guides, predicts that future celebrity chefs will be as likely to make their names in Vegas as in New York or Los Angeles.

meal along Paradise Road, adding to the options. Here, diners can choose from a plethora of major restaurants, locally-owned eateries, plus some small tasty ethnic cafes, all within walking distance of one another.

Away from the Strip and Downtown, chain franchises from fast food to pancake houses are now sucking up much of the local dining budget. But when the population of Vegas skyrocketed in the mid 1990s, some of the more upscale chains also made their way to the valley; for a town starved of choice for so long, this was manna from heaven.

Picasso restaurant at Bellagio

Home-Grown Talent

Locally-owned dining is also experiencing a boom, and many ethnic and specialty restaurants have opened. From the laid-back atmosphere of the Mediterranean Café (serving Middle Eastern specialties like falafel and hummous) to the homey environment of Chicago Joe's, and the artsy and elegant European vibe of Jazzed Café, the best medium-priced food is often outside the resort areas.

In fact, considering how rapidly the dining situation has improved – and the truckloads of money being spent to lure world-class chefs – Las Vegas may someday overtake all of its American rivals in the culinary sweepstakes.

HANDY TRAVEL TIPS

An A–Z Summary of Practical Information

A

ACCOMMODATIONS (See also CAMPING, YOUTH HOSTELS, and the list of RECOMMENDED HOTELS starting on page 125)

Las Vegas is a unique city in that the vast majority of its hotels offer both accommodations and attractions. Most of the places travelers want to see are found along the Strip or Downtown, so staying in one of these areas will put you right in the center of the action.

The quality of accommodations ranges from the best to the sleaziest, but most of the **hotel-casinos** fall comfortably into the average to above-average categories. Off-Strip hotel-casinos offer many of the same amenities – and sometimes more – as on-Strip hotels, and often at a lower price. Neighborhood hotel-casinos usually offer less in the way of amenities, but make up for it in price.

There are **non-gaming resorts** (such as the Alexis Park) if you prefer classy accommodations away from the clang of slot machines. Also, there are **non-gaming motels** all over the city, in the suburbs, and along Boulder Highway. Many of them specialize in extended stays of a week or more, and can be very good alternatives for travelers on a budget.

If you will be without a car, choose a hotel as close to your preferred action as possible. Las Vegas is spread widely, taxis are costly, and the public transportation system is not yet up to speed.

As there is no truly slow season in Las Vegas, room reservations are strongly advised, especially during the heavy travel periods in fall and spring and on any weekend, during major sporting events, for New Year's Eve, and whenever there is a major trade convention in town. In fact, some of the conventions draw over 200,000 people – enough to fill almost every room in the city. The **Las Vegas Convention and Visitors Authority**, tel: 702-892 0711, can alert you to when the events are in town. Travelers with internet access can search the LVCVA website at **<www.vegasfreedom.com>** or try **<www.vegas.com>**. If you have trouble finding a vacancy, try calling **Reservations Plus** at 1-800-805 9528 (toll-free in the US). Not only can they find and book you a room in your price range (often at a discount), they can also arrange entertainment packages as well. Best of all, the service is free.

There are still periods of relative quiet when rates are down and it is easier to find a room without reservations. The city is usually slower between Thanksgiving (fourth Thursday of November) and Christmas, as well as during the high-heat months of July and August. Then, room rates are up for grabs, and incredible bargains are to be had.

AIRPORT

Las Vegas is served by one major airport, McCarran International (tel: 702-261 5211). With the growth in travel to Las Vegas, the airport is among the country's busiest, and recently added 26 gates to handle the flow. The airport is also very close to town, within a 15-minute drive of Tropicana Avenue and the Strip. Transportation to and from the airport is available via an unending stream of taxis.

For a cheaper ride, try one of the shuttle buses that operate 24 hours and take you directly to your hotel for little money. One such company is **Bell Trans** (tel: 702-739 7990). There is also a public bus that serves the airport, but it takes significantly longer than the relatively inexpensive shuttle buses.

B

BICYCLE RENTAL

Bicycle riding within the city is not advised. For bicycle rental and tours of the surrounding natural areas by bicycle, call **Escape the City Streets** on 702-596 2953.

BUDGETING FOR YOUR TRIP

Las Vegas is one of the less expensive vacation destinations in the US – if you stay away from the tables. Once a flight has been paid for, everything else can be done on the cheap, from dining at a $5.99 all-you-can-eat buffet, to staying in a decent motel for as little as $20 per night. Sin City is a place that likes to do deals, and car rental firms and even major casinos often offer astonishingly low prices, usually in the hot summer months of July and August. If money is tight, it's worth deciding far in advance when you want to go, and shopping around on the web for competitive offers. Of course, it's also possible to spend a fortune in Vegas, especially if you take advantage of all the shopping and show opportunites; top shows like Cirque du Soliel charge over $100 per ticket. Museums and attractions have hefty admission prices, too, often around $15.

But the best way to lose money is to gamble. Setting and holding yourself to a budget is an important part of any trip to Las Vegas. Decide before leaving home exactly how much per day you have for gambling and do not permit yourself to exceed that amount; access to bank accounts via ATM cards is far too easy, and many only dole out $100s. More than a few travelers have arrived here happy, only to be forced to sell a prized possession for the fare home.

Tipping must be budgeted for as well. It is a recognized and accepted part of Las Vegas culture, and being unprepared can result in poor service (see TIPPING).

C

CAMPING

Within the city, there are plenty of RV parks as well as a **KOA** (tel: 702-451 5527) on Boulder Highway that has both RV and the only in-town tent sites. On the Strip, Circus Circus has a massive RV park, while many others exist beyond the Strip, such as those at Sam's Town and the Showboat, both on Boulder Highway.

Outside of the city, camping is plentiful in Red Rock Canyon, Lake Mead, and Mount Charleston, with Red Rock being only 15 minutes from the city *(see Excursions, page 64)*.

CAR RENTAL

Visitors who want any degree of freedom rent cars, and most do so at the airport on arrival. Advance reservations are suggested but not required. The local telephone directory lists 17 pages of rental agencies, all of the major US companies being represented (Alamo, Avis, Budget, Dollar, Enterprise, Hertz, National, and Thrifty), and rates are generally below the US average. The major companies usually won't rent to drivers under 25 years old, but some of the local companies will. All rental companies require a driver's license and a major credit card matching the license. Price quotes do not include taxes or liability and collision damage waivers (CDW). These can double the cost, so check with your credit card company to see what is already covered. No added insurance is required, but renters should weigh that choice carefully, since the heavy Las Vegas traffic is aggressive in nature.

CLIMATE

Las Vegas is a desert region, making summer temperatures very warm and dry and winters cold. August temperatures can reach over 115°F (46°C) in the mid-afternoon, and still hover around 100°F (38°C) at midnight. Winter temperatures can be surprisingly brisk, dipping very quickly after the sun sets. Spring is warmer but windy; fall is often the best time to visit, with warm days and mild nights. The sun shines an average of 305 days per year, so bring sunglasses and leave the umbrella at home.

	J	F	M	A	M	J	J	A	S	O	N	D
High												
°F	47	50	55	63	73	83	90	87	80	67	53	45
°C	8	10	13	17	23	28	32	31	27	19	17	7
Low												
°F	33	37	42	49	59	68	75	73	65	53	41	33
°C	0	3	6	9	15	20	24	23	18	17	7	0

CLOTHING

Requirements for dressing in Las Vegas have fluctuated over the years, from the formality of the 1940s through the 1960s to the T-shirts and shorts of the 1980s and 1990s. Today's styles range from upscale casual to downright shoddy, with everything imaginable in between. Little is out of place here, though remember that some nicer restaurants require jackets for men.

Remember also to pack clothing appropriate for the weather; short sleeves and skirts or shorts are accepted and nearly required for spending time outside in the summer months. Heavy winter jackets are what most winter visitors forget to pack, not expecting the chill of the winds that frequently assail the city. Sunblock is a must; a style-appropriate hat, or at least a pair of sunglasses, is highly recommended.

CRIME AND SAFETY

Las Vegas is a fairly safe place considering the high volume of tourist traffic with which it must contend. Hotel security is notoriously efficient (look up; the black-glass bubbles on the ceilings are a marker of security cameras monitored 24 hours a day), and Metro police bicycle patrols help curb problems along the Strip and Downtown. Still, standard big-city precautions should be taken. Avoid dark areas, especially Downtown. Pick-pocketing on city buses and in crowded areas – such as the Treasure Island pirate show or Bellagio's fountain display – is notorious, so watch your suitcases, purse, or wallet. In any emergency, dial 911 from any phone; no coins needed.

But visitors are much more likely to become a victim of an accident than they are a crime. Tourists walking down the Strip often become distracted by all the visual stimuli, so much so that between 1995 and 1997 134 pedestrians were killed by motorists. In many cases, the pedestrians were at fault, meandering into streets while looking at the lights, foolishly crossing the Strip's eight lanes of bumper-to-bumper traffic between lights, or simply backing into a lane of traffic while angling for a photograph. When walking in Las Vegas it is crucial to remember that, despite the temptation, you must not jaywalk or hop over barricades meant to prohibit pedestrian travel; otherwise you may be fined. Motorists are notoriously possessive of their travel lanes, and laws are set against pedestrians that violate the travel lane beyond a crosswalk.

CUSTOMS AND ENTRY FORMALITIES

Citizens of Canada and Mexico do not need visas or passports, but must show proof of residency. Citizens of most western European nations, as well as Australia, New Zealand, and Japan, can stay for up to 90 days without a visa, so long as they have a valid passport and a return air ticket. Others entering the US might need visas. Security arrangements since September 11, 2001, mean it's a good idea to carry proof of identity wherever you go.

Adult visitors staying longer than 72 hours may bring along the following items duty free: 1 liter of wine or liquor; 100 cigars (non-Cuban), or 3lbs (1.5kg) of tobacco, or 200 cigarettes (though they are so cheap here, one wonders why); and gifts valued under $100. Absolutely no food (including canned goods) or plants of any type are permissible. Visitors may also arrive and depart with up to $10,000 currency without declaration.

D

DRIVING

Driving can be a harrowing experience for anyone unused to city traffic. Las Vegas streets are busy and the drivers aggressive and unpredictable. Roads that are complete are in very good condition, owing to recent widening and paving. But there are many roadways under perpetual expansion and construction, making every day a new and frustrating experience.

Drive on the right side of the street. Right turns on red lights are permitted unless otherwise posted, as are U-turns. When a signal turns green, carefully check both directions before proceeding; Las Vegans are notorious for their attempts (and failures) to beat the traffic signal. Watch for school-crossing zones; fines are high and patrols are common. Do not drink and drive; penalties are stiff, and include immediate jail.

Freeways are the I-15 traveling north from Los Angeles to Salt Lake City, and US93/95, which comes from Arizona toward Utah.

Parking is easy, with every hotel offering free parking lots or structures (Downtown requires a casino cage validation). Valet parking is a free at-the-door service, but tips are customary. Remember that on busy nights, the valet may take longer to retrieve your car than you could have if you parked yourself (see TIPPING).

Gasoline is plentiful, available on nearly every corner and, though expensive by US standards, inexpensive compared to elsewhere in the world, especially Europe.

E

ELECTRIC CURRENT

All of the United States uses a 110-120 volt 50-cycle alternating current (AC). Transformers or plug adaptors are required for appliances using any other voltage, and are widely available.

EMERGENCIES

Dial **911** from any phone, toll-free.

G

GAY AND LESBIAN TRAVELERS

While Las Vegas may have a reputation as Sin City, it is only quietly tolerant of its fairly large gay and lesbian community, in the same look-the-other-way manner in which many gay entertainers have quietly been accepted. Many gay businesses, bars, and nightclubs are centered in the small, energetic Gay Triangle, an area off Paradise Road between Harmon and Tropicana. For information, pick up one of the free newspapers, *Las Vegas Bugle* or *Q-Tribe*, available at major record and bookstores.

GETTING THERE (see also AIRPORT and DRIVING)

There are only three modern methods of transportation available for passengers coming to Las Vegas: air, bus, or car, though there are plans to begin casino-sponsored train service from Los Angeles, which would arrive at the Downtown train station.

By Air

Las Vegas, though a major travel destination, is still considered a second-tier city when it comes to direct flights. While most major US cities, especially in the West, offer direct flights into McCarran International (the city's only major airport), many East Coast cities use hubs such as Denver, Chicago, and Phoenix. While some airlines add new direct flights on occasion, others withdraw theirs.

Direct, international flights come from Tokyo, Frankfurt, and London. Call the **Convention and Visitors Authority** at 702-892 0711 for information about international direct flights; call your airline regarding other flights.

By Bus

Greyhound Bus Lines offers daily bus travel to and from Las Vegas and surrounding cities. Call 1-800-231 2222 (toll-free in the US) for information.

GUIDES AND TOURS

Numerous tour operators are located in Las Vegas, and their advertisements can be seen in every free tourist guide available along the

Strip, as well as in hotel rooms. The majority of them specialize in tours of Southern Nevada's lake, mountains, Hoover Dam, and Boulder City, as well as bus and plane day-trips to the Grand Canyon *(see page 66)*.

Only a few companies specialize in tours of the city, taking busloads of sightseers past elaborate homes (or former homes) of stars, as well as attractions like the Ethel M. Chocolate Factory and the Fremont Street Experience. **Las Vegas Tour Center**, tel: 702-384 1234, offers several of these city tours, including a nearly nine-hour ride for around $30.

H

HEALTH AND MEDICAL CARE

Las Vegas is a modern city with modern health care and food standards. In the event of an emergency, there are seven area hospitals that provide 24-hour emergency care. Travelers needing medical attention in a non-emergency situation should seek out a **University Medical Center Quick Care** clinic, with seven citywide locations. They require no appointments, and accept any patient, but be prepared to wait up to an hour or two. If you have no health insurance (or insurance is not recognized), you will have to pay for medical services immediately.

Complementing this, there are several 24-hour pharmacies for prescription and non-prescription drugs. Both **Walgreen's** (Las Vegas Boulevard at Charleston Boulevard) and **White Cross Drugs** (farther north) are open 24 hours.

HOLIDAYS

Most businesses' opening hours are similar to public holidays. Hotel-casinos and resorts never close, regardless of the day or time, but grocery stores keep shorter hours on Christmas and Thanksgiving (fourth Thursday of November). Government offices, schools, the post office, and banks are closed for 11 national holidays. Holiday times are extremely busy at Las Vegas airport. The Fourth of July and Thanksgiving holidays really attract the crowds, with Christmas following closely behind.

M

MEDIA

Las Vegas has two daily **newspapers**: the morning *Review-Journal* and the afternoon *Sun*. The *R-J* has a more national orientation, while the *Sun* reads like the locally-owned metropolitan daily that it is. Hotel newsstands carry both, as well as the *New York Times, Los Angeles Times, USA Today,* and *Wall Street Journal*. For international newspapers, try Borders Bookshop, which has two locations.

There are a dozen **free local tourist guides**, ranging from small booklets of ads to more elaborate magazines with information content and listings. The two best are *What's On* and *Showbiz Weekly. What's On* is available in most hotel lobbies and on news racks, while *Showbiz* is found in hotel rooms throughout the city.

Las Vegas also has two **free alternative newsweeklies**, *CityLife* and the *Las Vegas Weekly*. They are available citywide in coffeehouses, cafes, bookstores, clubs, bars, and newspaper racks, and contain extensive listings of off-Strip information.

The valley's **television** is primarily served by Cox Communications cable system, with over 60 channels. Most hotel rooms have at least these stations: CNN, MTV, and USA networks, plus local affiliates ABC (channel 13), CBS (channel 8), FOX (channel 5), NBC (channel 3), and PBS (channel 10).

Radio has a full dial on both AM and FM bands. Highlights are KNPR (89.5FM, classical and NPR news), KUNV (91.5FM, jazz), KOMP (92.3FM, rock), KWNR (95.5FM, country-western), KXPT (97.1FM, classic and soft rock); KXTE (107.5FM, alternative rock), KDWN (720AM, talk), and KNEWS (970AM, news).

MONEY MATTERS

Currency. The monetary unit in the US, the dollar, is based on the decimal system, with 100 cents per dollar. The United States is converting its well-known paper currency to a bold new design, but compared to the old, it appears almost fake. If you aren't sure, ask a casino cage.

Common banknotes are in the $1, $5, $10, $20, $50, and $100 denominations. If you are unfamiliar with dollars, be careful handling them. The bills are all the same size and color, and the denominations can be hard to distinguish in low light. Mistakes can be costly. There are also silver dollar coins.

Currency exchange. While banks and other financial offices will exchange currency, there is no need; major casino cages will do so immediately and without commission. This is the first and best choice for exchanging cash.

Credit cards. It is strongly advised that you carry at least one major credit card with you while in Las Vegas. With the advent of checking-based Visa cards, their acceptance in stores, restaurants, and bars is nearly universal. You will still need some cash for tipping (see TIPPING).

Travelers' checks. Travelers' checks are accepted almost everywhere, though their relative complexity compared to credit cards makes them best for transporting cash between home and the casino cage, which will convert them into American currency as you require. You need to present your passport to exchange them for cash.

ATMs are accessible throughout all major casinos. Beware of additional service fees – often up to $2; these will be listed on the ATM itself.

Taxes. Taxation in Nevada is generally low in comparison to other US cities, thanks to heavy taxes on gaming revenue. Sales tax on merchandise and restaurant food is 7.25 percent; food (groceries) purchased in stores is exempt from sales tax. Lodging taxes are 7 percent, except Downtown, where taxes are 9 percent.

O

OPENING HOURS

Las Vegas is a 24-hour town. The hotel-casinos and most of the city's bars never close. Though all casinos have at least one 24-hour coffee shop, surprisingly, most restaurants keep shorter hours, closing by 10pm, 11pm on Saturday and Sunday. Retail stores and malls, both on- and off-Strip, open between 9 and 10am, closing at about 9pm (although some of the newer 'destination shopping centers', like the Forum Shops, open until midnight). Grocery and many drugstores are open 24 hours.

P

POLICE (see also CRIME AND SAFETY)

With 1.3 million residents and 30 million visitors annually, Las Vegas police take their work very seriously. They are generally helpful, and will guide tourists in the right direction if asked. Because of the traffic problems, however, they are unusully strict about jay-walking, so pedestrians should take particular care to observe signs, lights, and directions. Casually uniformed bicycle patrols on the Strip and Downtown have helped improve the public face of the LVPD. Call 911 in an emergency.

POST OFFICES

Local post offices are open 8am–5pm weekdays and 9am–1pm on Saturdays. There is one on Industrial Road behind the Stardust casino; use the main post office on Sunset Road if you need longer opening hours (6:30am–10pm Monday–Friday; 8am–4pm Saturday).

PUBLIC TRANSPORTATION

The main source of public transportation in Las Vegas is the **Citizens Area Transit** buses, or CAT for short. Buses along the Strip,

Downtown, and the Boulder Highway run 24 hours, while the 35 or so other citywide buses run 5:30am–1:30am, seven days a week. The central station for buses is the Downtown Transportation Center, tel: 702-228 7433, at Stewart and Casino Center, where you can get fare and schedule information. In 2003, a monorail system should help ease the traffic situation along the Strip, and hopes are that the monorail will eventually extend to Downtown.

T

TAXIS

Taxis are preferred by most tourists, but be warned: they are plentiful at all hotel *porte cacheres*, but nearly impossible to obtain by the streetside hailing method. You are better off walking up to a hotel and hiring one there. Further, calling a cab from a far-flung distance often requires up to an hour-long wait (see also TIPPING).

TELEPHONE

The country code for the US is 1; the area code for Clark County (where Las Vegas is located) is 702. While in the Vegas area, calls to the metropolitan vicinity require only the seven-digit number. Beyond the area but still in Nevada, dial 1 + 702 + (the seven-digit number). Out-of-state-calls require 1 + (area code) + (number). International calls require 011 + (country code) + (city code) + (number). Be aware that hotels hike up the price of calls enormously.

TICKETS

Hotels have their own box offices, many of which accept over-the-phone purchases with a credit card. Tickets for some hotel events, as well as most other major events in Las Vegas (concerts, sporting events) can be purchased via **Ticketmaster** at 702-474 4000. Remember, there are surcharges for using ticketing services, so prices will be cheaper if you buy direct from the venue's box office.

TIME DIFFERENCES

The US is divided into four time zones; Las Vegas is in the Pacific Standard Time Zone, which is eight hours behind Greenwich Mean Time. Las Vegas operates on Daylight Savings Time; in late April, clocks move ahead by one hour, and then fall back by one hour in late October.

Las Vegas	New York	London	Jo'burg	Sydney
9am	12pm	5pm	7pm	3am (next day)

TIPPING

Tipping is the grease that keeps the machine of Las Vegas operating, far more than in other American cities. Most tourist service employees depend on tips as an important portion of their income. Tipping is simpler and less trouble if you carry a selection of dollars in the $1, $5, and $10 denominations with you for this purpose.

Most tipping is in the $1–$3 range, but sometimes a larger tip will help things move along. No table available at a big hotel restaurant for hours? A $10 or $20 bill will usually get you a seat immediately. Valet parking full? Try $5 first, more if it is a holiday or special event, and a space will often magically appear. If at valet pick-up a huge group of people are already waiting for their cars, waits of up to 20 minutes are not uncommon; however, a bill with the right picture on it handed to the ticket taker with a request to speed up the process will almost always have you out pretty quickly. When you tip under these circumstances, do so discreetly.

Restaurant tipping ranges between 15 to 20 percent of the total bill before taxes. A good tipper will go to 20 percent for extraordinary service. Be warned: some restaurants automatically include a 12 to 15 percent surcharge for large tables; you may argue the charge if service is poor. If it *is* included, you may of course add a small percentage for exceptional service. Remember, if service is bad, you are not obligated to tip, but select another server the next time you visit that establishment. Here are some general suggestions, but when in doubt, always overtip: in Las Vegas, this may improve your vacation immeasurably:

Bartenders	$1–$2 per round for two or more
Bellmen	$1 per bag
Cocktail Waitresses	$1–$2 per round
Concierges	$1 and up, depending upon service
Doormen	$1 per bag, $1 for cab call
Limo Drivers	15 percent of total bill
Maids	$1–$2 per day, left at the end of stay
Pool Attendants	$1
Taxi Drivers	20 percent
Valet Parking	$1–$2 when car is returned; $5–$10 to find a spot on a busy night; $5 to ticket taker for fast return
Wait Staff (Restaurant)	15–20 percent of total before taxes
Wait Staff (Showroom)	$5–$10

Tipping in Casinos

Change Attendants	5 percent and up, depending on your luck and their interaction
Cocktail Waitresses	$1, particularly if the drink is free; tipping with gaming chips is acceptable as well.
Dealers	If you are winning, tip the dealer by placing a bet for him or her, one-half of your bet; when leaving the table in the black, tip according to your conscience

TOURIST INFORMATION OFFICES

Contact the **Las Vegas Convention and Visitors Authority** for tourist information at 3150 Paradise Road, Las Vegas, NV 89109, tel: 702-892 0711.

W

WEBSITES AND ON-LINE RESOURCES

Internet cafes can be hard to find in the US compared to Europe. The nearest equivalent is usually an office bureau like Kinko's, which offer access, but at a high cost. Access can also sometimes be found at mini-market food stores along the Strip.

Public libraries in Las Vegas offer internet access at little or no charge. The Las Vegas Library is at 833 Las Vegas Boulevard North, tel: 702-507 3600. There are also facilities in most hotel business centers, though these are expensive.

If you want to investigate Las Vegas on-line before you leave home, the following are some websites to help you do it:

<www.vegasfreedom.com> The official website of the Las Vegas Visitors and Convention Authority.

<www.vegas.com> Operated by the parent company of the *Las Vegas Sun, Showbiz Weekly, Las Vegas Life,* and *Las Vegas Weekly,* this is perhaps the most comprehensive collection of original news and information about the city on the net.

<www.lasvegas.com> Hosted by the competitors of vegas.com, this fairly comprehensive site features news from the *Las Vegas Review-Journal,* plus community partner links to numerous local agencies and institutions; especially useful for relocation.

<www.hiddenvegas.com> Maintained by a former journalist, this site has a guide to local alternative culture as well as links to cultural websites and those with other – more edgy – Vegas material.

Y

YOUTH HOSTELS

There is only one hostel, the **Las Vegas International Hostel** (tel: 702-385 9955) between the Strip and Downtown. The neighborhood is not the best, but safe during the day; travel in pairs at night.

Recommended Hotels

There are at least 130,000 hotel rooms in Las Vegas. This makes selecting accommodations intimidating, but not impossible. Consider the usual factors – cost, location, and budget – as well as how integral you want your hotel to be to your visit. It is possible, though not advisable, to visit Las Vegas and never leave your hotel premises.

The following is a recommended selection of Sin City's best hotels in four price categories. For a comprehensive listing of available hotels and motels, call the Las Vegas Convention and Visitors Authority (see ACCOMMODATIONS on page 109).

All businesses must comply with the 'Americans with Disabilities' Act, and so are wheelchair accessible. Newer properties are the easiest to navigate, older and Downtown properties slightly more difficult. All hotels accept all major credit cards (Visa, Mastercard, American Express), but price ranges listed do not include suites. Expect holiday and weekend rates to be significantly higher, and be sure to ask for specific quotes for your intended stay, a special package deal can cut costs considerably. For more information about most of these hotels, particularly with regard to their casinos and attractions, look in WHERE TO GO starting on page 27.

$$$$	over $200
$$$	$100–$200
$$	$50–$100
$	under $50

STRIP CASINOS AND RESORTS

Aladdin Resort and Casino $$$ *3667 Las Vegas Boulevard South, tel: 702-785 5555, toll free: 1-877-333 WISH, fax: 702-736 7101 <www.aladdincasino.com>*. Built on the site of its old namesake, and with an 'Enchanted Garden.' The guest bathrooms are particularly generous. Theme: Arabia. 2,567 rooms.

Bally's Hotel and Casino $$$ *3645 Las Vegas Boulevard South, tel: 702-739 4111, toll free: 1-800-634 3434, fax: 702-967 4405 <www.ballyslv.com>*. Bally's is one of the oldest hotels on the Strip, but also one of the most overlooked, and therefore the nicest. Large rooms with a modern flair feature overstuffed furniture and subdued earth-tones. The hotel has a beautiful pool area that is perfect for hot days. 2,814 rooms.

Barbary Coast $$$ *3595 Las Vegas Boulevard South, tel: 702-737 7111, toll free: 1-888-227 2279, fax: 702-894 9954 <www.barbarycoastcasino.com>*.Wedged in a corner of Las Vegas Boulevard between Bally's and the Flamingo, the rooms here offer a charming and comfortable rendition of the 'City by the Bay' *circa* 1900, featuring brass beds and etched mirrors. A big draw of the hotel-casino is the recently added restaurant, Drai's. Theme: Old San Francisco. 200 rooms.

Bellagio Hotel and Casino $$$$ *3600 Las Vegas Boulevard South, tel: 702-693 7111, toll free: 1-888-987 6667, fax: 702-792 7646 <www.bellagioresort.com>*. The city's most lavish resort, Bellagio proves what kind of Italian replication $1.6 billion can buy. The standard guest rooms are satisfyingly plush, decorated in shades of brown, black, and cream. Two key perks are the comfortable beds and huge bathrooms with deep-soaking tubs and showers big enough for two. Tip: be sure to ask for a room overlooking the fountains, as there is in-room music on the TV dial that is choreographed to the water show. Theme: Italian/Mediterranean elegance. 3,005 rooms, with more to come in a new spa tower.

Caesars Palace Hotel and Casino $$$ *3570 Las Vegas Boulevard South, tel: 702-731 7110, toll free: 1-800-634 6661, fax: 702-731 7172 <www.caesars.com>*. A standard-setter since its opening, elegance at Caesars seems within reach of anyone. A recent renovation–including a new tower and pool–raises the level of its already excellent accommodations, where marble and mahogany abound. Baths feature oversize marble tubs and European fixtures, and rooms are tastefully decorated with art and sculpture. Theme: ancient Rome. 2,454 rooms.

Circus Circus Hotel and Casino $$ *2880 Las Vegas Boulevard South, tel: 702-734 0410, toll free: 1-800-444 2472, fax: 702-734 5897 <www.circuscircus.com>*. Circus Circus is Las Vegas's original family-friendly, low-roller hotel-casino. The renovated lobby is classy, but you cannot expect Strip accommodations at this price without compromise. Rooms are typical chain hotel style, with blue carpeting and blonde wood furniture. To stay in the newer rooms, request one in the West Tower. Theme: the Big Top, though not in the rooms. 3,744 rooms.

Excalibur Hotel and Casino $$ *3850 Las Vegas Boulevard South, tel: 702-597 7777, toll free: 1-800-937 7777, fax: 702-597 7009 <www.excaliburcasino.com>*. Excalibur offers a Renaissance Faire experience aimed squarely at families and travelers on a budget. Rooms are surprisingly restrained considering the hotel's gaudy exterior, with wrought-iron accents over dark wood and contemporary touches of red, blue, and green. Theme: Medieval Fantasy. 4,008 rooms.

Flamingo Hilton Las Vegas $$$ *3555 Las Vegas Boulevard South, tel: 702-733 3111, toll free: 1-800-732 2111, fax: 702-733 3353 <www.flamingolv.com>*. The Flamingo retains its original desert oasis flavor with a large, lush tropical pool and garden area. Most rooms in the six towers have recognizably Hilton decor, with tropical accents highlighting conservative colors and rattan furniture. 3,530 rooms.

Four Seasons Hotel Las Vegas $$$$ *3960 Las Vegas Boulevard South, tel: 702-632 5000 or 877-632 5200 <www.fourseasons.com>*. The Four Seasons offers quiet, ultra-luxurious accommodations on the upper floors of the Mandalay Bay tower, accessed only via a private-lobby elevator. The two-story main building houses the lobby, four restaurants and bars, a health spa, and meeting rooms. A large pool set in a lush garden is available only to Four Seasons guests. 424 rooms.

Harrah's Las Vegas $$$ *3475 Las Vegas Boulevard South, tel: 702-369 5000, toll free: 1-800-427 7247, fax: 702-369 5008.*

Harrah's recently underwent a $200-million renovation; the newest rooms are in the 35-story tower. Bright colors, light wood, and brass fixtures lend an upbeat feel to the accommodations. Jacuzzi tubs are available. Theme: Carnival. 2,613 rooms.

Holiday Inn Boardwalk $$ *3750 Las Vegas Boulevard South, tel: 702-735 2400, toll free: 1-800-635 4581, fax: 702-739 8152 <www.hiboardwalk.com>*. People who prefer the familiarity of a hotel chain will like the Holiday Inn on the Strip. Request a room in the recently completed tower; furnished with cherrywood and bright colors, they are nicer than the older rooms. Theme: vague Coney Island. 654 rooms.

Imperial Palace Hotel and Casino $$ *3535 Las Vegas Boulevard South, tel: 702-731 3311, toll free: 1-800-634 6441, fax: 702-735 8578 <www.imperialpalace.com>*. This sprawling complex houses quite a few average but comfortable rooms. The adventurous can rent a suite with a mirrored Jacuzzi tub and mirrored ceiling over the bed, while the pool area with tumbling waterfall is large and beautiful. Theme: Oriental Palace. 2,700 rooms.

Luxor Hotel and Casino $$–$$$ *3900 Las Vegas Boulevard South, tel: 702-262 4000, toll free: 1-800-288 1000, fax: 702-262 4404 <www.luxor.com>*. The Luxor consists of a 30-story Egyptian pyramid and two towers. The rooms in the pyramid have one sloping glass wall overlooking the main floor, and most have a shower but no tub (rooms in the towers do have tubs). The rooms feature art deco and Egyptian-inspired furnishings, with marble bathrooms. Many family-friendly attractions are here, and discount rates are often available. Theme: ancient Egypt. 4,400 rooms.

Mandalay Bay Resort and Casino $$$ *3950 Las Vegas Boulevard South, tel: 702-632 7777 or 877-632 7000 <www.mandalaybay.com>*. Guests at the Mandalay will enjoy an 11-acre (4-hectare) tropical environment, including a wave pool, an enormous spa, and a number of trendy restaurants, including the House of Blues. Theme: luxurious urban tropical jungle. 3,300 rooms, plus a new tower and a convention center.

MGM Grand Hotel and Casino $$$ *3799 Las Vegas Boulevard South, tel: 702-891 7777, toll free: 1-800-929 1111, fax: 702-891 1030 <www.mgmgrand.com>*. Four distinct towers result in four different types of room themes. The nicest are in the Hollywood tower, with gold-speckled walls surrounding maple and cherry furniture. Gilded accents and framed photos of classic film stars add up to the classy experience. The other towers–Casablanca, Old South, and Oz–feature rooms that also relate to their names. Theme: City of Entertainment. 5,034 rooms.

Mirage Hotel and Casino $$$ *3400 Las Vegas Boulevard South, tel: 702-791 7111, toll free: 1-800-627 6667, fax: 702-791 7414 <www.mirage.com>*. A lovely Polynesian resort, despite being the oldest of the city's post-1950s additions. The rooms have a distinctive beach resort feel, with subdued neutral colors and gold accents. Most have marbled entries and baths, as well as canopied beds. Though the rooms are somewhat small, they are among the nicest on the Strip. Theme: South Seas. 3,000 rooms.

Monte Carlo Hotel and Casino $$$ *3770 Las Vegas Boulevard South, tel: 702-730 7777, toll free: 1-800-311 8999, fax: 702-730 7250 <www.monte-carlo.com>*. Striking in its understated European theme, this resort captures an air of popular beauty. The outdoor area is particularly lush, with a wave pool, waterfalls, and a river. Rooms are classically European in flavor and very comfortable. Theme: old-Europe elegance. 3,200 rooms.

New York-New York Hotel and Casino $$$ *3790 Las Vegas Boulevard South, tel: 702-740 6969, toll free: 1-888-696 9887, fax: 702-740 6700 <www.nynyhotelcasino.com>*. Taking theming to its extreme, rooms here are done in 62 unique styles, all related to the 'Big Apple.' Art deco is the overall inspiration, with round-top furnishings and inlaid wood galore. On average, the rooms (and their bathrooms) are small, but the overall experience is pleasant. Theme: New York City. 2,034 rooms.

Paris Hotel and Casino $$$ *3655 Las Vegas Boulevard South, tel: 702-946 7000, toll free: 1-888-266 5687, fax: 702-946 4405*

<www.paris-lv.com>. Paris Las Vegas is modeled after the City of Light's Hôtel de Ville, with numerous replicas of Parisian landmarks, including the Eiffel Tower, Rue de la Paix, the Paris Opera House, the Louvre, and the Arc de Triomphe. Food – as you would expect – is excellent. Theme: classic France. 2,916 rooms.

Riviera Hotel and Casino $$ *2901 Las Vegas Boulevard South, tel: 702-734 5110, toll free: 1-800-634 6753, fax: 702-794 9451 <www.theriviera.com>*. One of the older Strip resorts, the Monaco and Monte Carlo towers house the newest, nicest rooms, each richly decorated with mahogany furniture and burgundy fabrics. Most tower rooms offer views of the pool or mountains; the scenery from the original nine-story structure is less rewarding. 2,100 rooms.

Sahara Hotel and Casino $$ *2535 Las Vegas Boulevard South, tel: 702-737 2111, toll free: 1-888-696 2121, fax: 702-791 2027 <www.stardustlv.com>*. A recent $100-million renovation went the usual Vegas route, replacing a dark and plush atmosphere with lighter decor. The result is one of attractive comfort for tour groups, conventioneers, and mid-budget travelers. Rooms are bright, utilizing lots of earth-tones and wood. Theme: Moroccan Palace. 1,758 rooms.

Stardust Resort and Casino $$ *3000 Las Vegas Boulevard South, tel: 702-732 6111, toll free: 1-800-634 6757, fax: 702-732 6296*. Think of the Stardust as an adult-oriented gambling playground. The newest guest rooms are in the two towers: the west tower decor consists of earth-tones with black accents, while the east tower rooms have lighter colors and floral prints. Guest rooms are comfortable, though not very exciting. 2,500 rooms.

Stratosphere Hotel and Casino $$ *2000 Las Vegas Boulevard South, tel: 702-380 7777, toll free: 1-800-998 6937, fax: 702-383 5334*. Unfortunately, there are no rooms in the big tower. Instead, accommodations are located in one of the mid-rise towers. Rooms are surprisingly comfortable, nicely decorated with art deco touches and black lacquer. The semi-central location, however – not quite the Strip, not quite Downtown – leaves the Stratosphere out on its own. 1,444 rooms.

Treasure Island $$$ *3300 Las Vegas Boulevard South, tel: 702-894 7111, toll free: 1-800-944 7444, fax: 702-894 7414 <www.treasureisland.com>*. Affordable and comfortable–though not elaborate–rooms are housed in a Y-shaped tower. The Caribbean theme is pervasive, and colors are similar to the casino: parchment and washed yellows. Rooms on the Strip face the Pirate Battle, though the view might be obscured. Other rooms look out over the Mirage casino or the mountains. Theme: Pirates of the Caribbean. 2,900 rooms.

Tropicana Resort and Casino $$$ *3801 Las Vegas Boulevard South, tel: 702-739 2222, toll free: 1-800-634 4000, fax: 702-739 2469 <www.tropicanalv.com>*. Aimed at adult travelers, the hotel is a slice of subtly-themed Polynesia – bamboo and wood dominate. Guest rooms in the Island tower have a tropical theme, while the Paradise tower's rooms lean toward French Provincial. The tropical pool area (with swim-up blackjack tables) is lush and relaxing. Theme: low-key Hawaiian. 2,000 rooms.

The Venetian Resort Hotel-Casino $$$ *3355 Las Vegas Boulevard South, tel: 702-414 1000, toll free: 1-888-283 6423, fax: 702-414 4800 <www.venetian.com>*. Renaissance Italy is captured in dramatic architecture and landscaping, including canals with operating gondolas. A four-level entertainment plaza includes a showroom, and the Grand Canal Shoppes contain 140 stores and restaurants. Theme: traditional Venice. 3,354 rooms, plus a new tower.

DOWNTOWN CASINOS AND RESORTS

Binion's Horseshoe Hotel and Casino $$ *128 Fremont Street, tel: 702-382 1600, toll free: 1-800-237 6537, fax: 702-382 5750.* The Horseshoe may be the most traditional gambling joint left in town. Its flocked-wallpaper-and-velvet-drapes ambiance surrounds the highest betting limits in the world, and the comfortable accommodations are modestly priced. 380 rooms.

California Hotel and Casino $$ *12 Ogden Avenue, tel: 702-385 1222, toll free: 1-800-634 6505, fax: 702-388 2610*

<*www.thecal.com*>. This hotel draws guests mostly from Hawaii and Asia, though all visitors are welcome. The California's decor offers a taste of the South Seas rather than the Wild West; the rooms, however, are more contemporary in style, complete with marble baths. Located off Fremont Street. 781 rooms.

El Cortez Hotel and Casino $ *600 Fremont Street, tel: 702-385 5200, toll free: 1-800-634 6703, fax: 702-385 1554* <*www.jackie-gaughan.com*>. El Cortez (built in 1941) is the city's oldest operating casino–and unabashedly proletariat. The most pleasant rooms are in the 14-story tower, but the old rooms are still charming, with nice, wood floors. Everything is clean and comfortable, but do not expect extravagance. 402 rooms.

Fitzgerald's Casino Hotel $$ *301 Fremont Street, tel: 702-388 2400, toll free: 1-800-274 5825, fax: 702-388 2478* <*www.fitzgeralds.com*>. Many of the Fitzgerald's rooms offer nice views of the city and mountains within comfortable surroundings. Accommodations are of the standard Holiday Inn variety (in fact, they *are* Holiday Inn rooms), and within a mid-budget price range. Attractive views of the Fremont Street Experience can also be enjoyed in this (mostly) low-roller haven. 638 rooms.

4 Queens Hotel and Casino $$ *202 Fremont Street, tel: 702-385 4011, toll free: 1-800-634 6045, fax: 702-387 5185* <*www.fourqueens.com*>. A neon landmark since 1966, the 4 Queens today entices mainly older guests. Rooms are of Southwestern or earth-tone decor and are pleasant and affordable. Four restaurants include Hugo's Cellar, an always-busy classic Las Vegas gourmet room with an award-winning wine list. 690 rooms.

Fremont Hotel and Casino $$ *200 East Fremont Street, tel: 702-385 3232, toll free: 1-800-634 6460, fax: 702-385 6229* <*www.fremontcasino.com*>. Constructed in 1956 as Las Vegas's first high-rise building, the Fremont's guest rooms are comfortable, modern, and decorated in a tropical-floral style. The hotel hosts many Hawaiian travelers and so the Second Street Grill features Pacific Rim specialties. 452 rooms.

Golden Gate Hotel and Casino $ *1 Fremont Street, tel: 702-385 1906, toll free: 1-800-426 1906, fax: 702-383 9681.* This charming operation is one of the city's oldest hotels, and perhaps the only bed-and-breakfast experience in Las Vegas. Its small (10 sq ft/3 sq m) but elegant rooms, with plaster walls and mahogany doors, hark back to another era. 106 rooms.

Golden Nugget $$$ *129 East Fremont Street, tel: 702-385 7111, toll free: 1-800-634 3454, fax: 702-386 8362.* The 1946 Golden Nugget is the jewel of Downtown; metropolitan elegance supersedes the surrounding glitz. Guests, greeted by uniformed doormen, enter a gilded lobby full of marble and crystal. Accommodations – featuring a misted pool area landscaped with palms – are luxurious enough to have earned a top AAA rating. 1.907 rooms.

Lady Luck Casino Hotel $$ *206 North Third Street, tel: 702-477 3000, toll free: 1-800-523 9582, fax: 702-366 9602 <www.ladyluck.com>.* The rooms here – especially in the two newer towers – are very comfortable. The hotel-casino has two rarities that are more like the Strip than Downtown – a showroom staging a production magic show, and a swimming pool. 791 rooms.

Main Street Station $$ *200 North Main Street, tel: 702-387 1896, toll free: 1-800-713 8933, fax: 702-386 4466 <www.mainstreetcasino.com>.* Main Street Station is Las Vegas's best-kept secret, as the Victorian-styled casino is filled with expensive antiques. Rooms are spacious, quiet, and simply decorated, with shutters instead of drapes. Dining options include several very good restaurants. 406 rooms.

Plaza Hotel and Casino $ *1 Main Street, tel: 702-386 2110, toll free: 1-800-634 6575, fax: 702-382 8281 <plazahotelcasino.com>.* A few steps from the Greyhound bus station and seen in almost all photographs of neon-lit Downtown, this high-rise hotel has its own wedding chapel as well as exercise facilities, a swimming pool, three restaurants, a concierge desk, cable TV, and even a shuttle to the airport. Great value for the price. 1,000 rooms.

OFF-STRIP CASINOS AND RESORTS

Alexis Park $$$ *375 East Harmon, tel: 702-796 3330, toll free: 1-800-582 2228, fax: 702-796 4334.* A Mediterranean villa on 20 acres (8 hectares) of beautifully landscaped grounds, this resort offers volumes beyond the typical Las Vegas hotel. Styled with classy European elegance, all rooms are suites, with 10 distinct floor plans and different decor throughout. A lack of gaming means the place is noticeably quiet, but the Alexis is directly across from the Hard Rock Hotel and Casino if you're in the mood to hit the tables. 500 rooms.

Boulder Station Hotel and Casino $$ *4111 Boulder Highway, 89121, tel: 702-432 7777, toll free: 1-800-683 7777, fax: 702-432 7744 <www.boulderstation.com>*. Located on the Boulder Strip going out of town, the Boulder Station Hotel offers a small-scale version of the inclusive upscale resort. Rooms are comfortable and attractive, but a bit higher-priced than many other off-Strip resorts. 300 rooms.

Gold Coast Hotel and Casino $$ *4000 West Flamingo Road, tel: 702-367-7111, toll free: 1-888-402 6278, fax: 702-385 7505.* The Gold Coast Hotel offers a combination of entertainment and gaming, as well as a bowling center, three lounges, a dance hall, and a theater. Guest rooms are both comfortable and affordable. 711 rooms.

Hard Rock Hotel and Casino $$$ *4455 Paradise Road, tel: 702-693 5000, toll free: 1-800-693 7625, fax: 702-693 5010 <www.hardrockhotel.com>*. A surprising exercise in casual elegance, the Hard Rock's rooms are spacious and pleasing, decorated in a classic Modernist style. Light fixtures made of cymbals adorn the ceilings. All bedrooms have balconies, though the ones with a pool views are preferable. Theme: rock and roll. 700 rooms.

Las Vegas Hilton Hotel and Casino $$$ *3000 South Paradise Road, tel: 702-732 5111, toll free: 1-888-732 7117, fax: 702-732 5805 <www.lv-hilton.com>*. Located next to the Convention Center, the Hilton does brisk business during large conventions. The lobby and casino are gracious and expensively outfitted, and the already plush guest rooms – each loaded with overstuffed chairs, large closets, and marble-tiled bathrooms – recently underwent a complete renovation. 3,174 rooms.

Orleans Hotel and Casino $$ *4500 West Tropicana Avenue, tel: 702-365 7111, toll free: 1-800-675 3267, fax: 702-365 7505.* The guest rooms here are among the city's largest, and are often an excellent bargain. They are lavishly appointed, with decor in brass, antiques, and lace. Theme: the Big Easy. 840 rooms.

Palace Station Hotel and Casino $$ *2411 West Sahara Avenue, tel: 702-367 2411, toll free: 1-800-634 3101, fax: 702-367 2478.* Located just off the Strip near Interstate 15, the Palace Station's best rooms are within the tower, built in 1991, while original rooms are in a two-story building surrounding the pool. If possible, request one of the corner rooms, which have larger bathrooms. 1,030 rooms.

Rio All-Suites Hotel and Casino $$$ *3700 West Flamingo Road, tel: 702-252 7777, toll free: 1-800-752 9746, fax: 702-252 8909.* The Rio offers such quality that it has received international acclaim (it's one of the city's best values). The newer accommodations are in the Masquerade Tower, but even standard rooms are still well on the large side. Decor is a contemporary style of bold colors and wood. 2,556 rooms.

Sam's Town Hotel and Casino $$ *5111 Boulder Highway, 89122, tel: 702-456 7777, toll free: 1-800-634 6371, fax: 702-454 8017 <www.samstown.com>.* The rustic Wild West and Native American decor may sound kitschy, but the rooms here are actually quiet, comfortable, and attractive. The real treat is the nine-story atrium over an indoor park, complete with live trees, running water, and footpaths. Some in-facing rooms below the ninth floor are within this atrium. 650 rooms.

Sunset Station $$ *1301 West Sunset Road, 89119, tel: 702-547 7777, toll free: 1-888-319 4655, fax: 702-547 7744 <www.sunsetstation.com>.* The Mediterranean interior of the Sunset Station is really quite stunning. Amenities include a 13-screen movie theater and KidsQuest indoor play area, making this a sure-fire family winner. Sunset Sation is located far off the Strip in Green Valley, across from a major shopping area. 450 rooms.

MOTELS

City Center Motel $ *700 East Fremont Street, tel: 702-382 4766, fax: 702-382-9937.* This 58-room Downtown motel has a pool, a sundeck, and a restaurant directly across the street.

Days Inn Downtown $ *707 East Fremont Street, tel: 702-388 1400, toll free: 1-800-325 2344, fax: 702-388 9622.* This chain motel has an elevated pool, a sundeck, a restaurant, and even its own slot-machine parlor.

Howard Johnson $-$$ *1401 Las Vegas Boulevard, tel: 702-388 0301, toll free: 1-800-307 7199, fax: 702-388 2506 <www.hojo.com>.* Located near the Convention Center, this motel has an Olympic-size pool, a restaurant, and a wedding chapel.

King Albert Motel $ *185 Albert Avenue, tel: 702-732 1555, toll free: 1-800-553 7753.* This budget-priced motel off the Strip has a swimming pool, a laundromat, and kitchenettes.

Motel 6 $ *195 East Tropicana Avenue, tel: 702-798 0728.* Three blocks from the Strip and not far from the airport, this motel has a swimming pool, a food store, and plenty of parking.

Motel 8 $ *3961 Las Vegas Boulevard South, tel: 702-798 7223.* Basic accommodations in an excellent location, opposite the Mandalay Bay and near the action.

Viva Las Vegas $ *1205 Las Vegas Boulevard South, tel: 702-384 0771, toll free: 1-800-574 4450 <www.vivalasvegasvillas.com>.* Funky, light-hearted 'themed' motel near the Stratosphere Tower. Rooms are clean and comfortable. If you get married in the wedding chapel, 'Elvis' may participate or even officiate.

Recommended Restaurants

Restaurants here are listed alphabetically and according to location. Price ranges are per person for a typical entree in that part of Las Vegas. Outstanding buffets are listed in this section, with the name of the hotel first. Expect to stand in line (and pay) for a buffet before you enter. Once inside, you can eat all you wish, though it is considered unacceptable to bring food out of the buffet area. Soft drinks are often included in the price of the buffet, but beer and wine is purchased separately at the register. A tip is usually left on the table after the meal. For more information about the dining scene in Las Vegas, see EATING OUT on page 104.

All of the restaurants listed below accept all major credit cards (Visa, Mastercard, and American Express).

$$$$	$30 and over
$$$	$25–$30
$$	$13–$24
$	under $12

STRIP RESTAURANTS

Bertolini's $$ *Caesars Palace Forum Shops, tel: 702-735 4663.* Lunch and dinner. This upscale franchise offers delicious Italian entrees and wood-fired pizza. Most patrons choose to dine 'outdoors' near a huge (and loud) fountain.

Canaletto $–$$$$ *Venetian Grand Canal Shoppes, tel: 702-414 4500.* Lunch and dinner. Although the food at Canaletto is pleasant, the experience of dining by the waterside while sitting in the middle of a desert is the one to write home about.

Cheesecake Factory $$ *Caesars Palace Forum Shops, tel: 702-792 6888.* Breakfast, lunch, and dinner. The Factory is a cavernous restaurant with a huge menu offering a variety of food. Sunday brunch (not buffet) is delicious. Though you'll be tempted to sit mall-side, don't – the statue water show is pretty noisy and can be disruptive.

Chinois $$$ *Caesars Palace Forum Shops, tel: 702-737 9700.* Lunch and dinner. A Wolfgang Puck creation, this one by the celebrity chef is an upscale Pan-Asian affair where diners enjoy selections from an innovative Pacific Rim menu. The cafe section is substantially less expensive than the dining room.

Coyote Cafe and Grill Room $$$ *MGM Grand, tel: 702-891 7349.* Breakfast, lunch, and dinner. Mark Miller's Coyote Cafe serves inspired Southwestern-nouvelle and delicious chili-filled dishes. Avoid the cafe; the good food is served in the grill.

Drai's $$$ *Barbary Coast; tel: 702-737 7111.* Dinner only. Restaurateur to the stars in Hollywood, Victor Drai's eatery has made the Barbary Coast Hotel a great place to eat. The menu is elaborate French nouvelle, and the appetizers are delicious.

Emeril's $$$ *MGM Grand, tel: 702-891 7374.* Lunch and dinner. Seafood was almost unheard of in the desert until Emeril Lagasse arrived. Imaginative preparations result in amazingly delicate dining experiences, with a great wine list to top it all off.

Mirage Buffet $ *The Mirage, tel: 702-891 7374.* Breakfast, lunch, and dinner. An excellent, all-you-can-eat feast. Though a little expensive, the overall quality, fabulous salad selection, and delicious desserts make this a winner.

Noodles $$ *Bellagio, tel: 702-693 8131.* Lunch and dinner. A modern Tony Chi-designed Pan-Asian noodle shop in the heart of Las Vegas. The Modernist touches are elegantly trendy, and the variety of menu selections vast and authentic.

Palm $$$$ *Caesars Palace Forum Shops, tel: 702-732 7256.* Lunch and dinner. A steakhouse of near perfection that also serves lobster. The wine list is extensive,with many by-the-glass choices.

Picasso $$$$ *Bellagio, tel: 702-693 7223.* Dinner only. The French cooking of master chef Julian Serrano has ensured that Picasso is now a restaurant of not just local, but national importance. While you're waiting for the next culinary treat, admire the art on the walls. They really are by that other, even more famous, master.

Spago $$$ *Caesars Palace Forum Shops, tel: 702-369 6300.* Lunch and dinner. One of the first Los Angeles eateries to introduce fusion cooking techniques, Wolfgang Puck's Las Vegas restaurant is as much about being seen there as it is eating there. A French-, Asian-, and Italian-inspired menu ends with fabulous desserts.

Top of the World $$$$ *Stratosphere Tower, tel: 702-380 7777.* Lunch and dinner. The food often takes second place here, as the revolving restaurant offers diners a full-circle view of Las Vegas every hour. Though the view is unparalleled, the continental cuisine is not bad either.

Tre Visi $$ *MGM Grand, tel: 702-891 7220.* Breakfast, lunch, and dinner. An informal cafe attached to a more formal dining room, this pair turns the tables on any expectations. The cafe is the more desirable of the two, featuring delicious Tuscan specialties and light and flavorful pizzas.

DOWNTOWN RESTAURANTS

Bay City Diner $ *Golden Gate Hotel, tel: 702-382 3510.* Open 24 hours a day. The Bay City Diner is a 24-hour cafe with a twist. A dark wood interior and turn-of-the-20th century feel lend a pleasant ambiance to accompany the standard coffee shop menu.

Binion's Ranch Steakhouse $$$ *Binion's Horseshoe, tel: 702-382 1600.* Dinner only. Some of the best beef in the West comes through this steakhouse (the Binions are ranchers as well as casino-owners). The 24th-floor view of the city is pleasant, too.

Garden Court Buffet $ *Main Street Station, tel: 702-387 1896.* A beautiful, relaxing buffet experience set under high ceilings, surrounded by marble and brick. Multiple food stations allow hungry diners to sample everything from wood-fired pizzas to Mexican and Asian specialties.

Hugo's Cellar $$$ *4 Queens, tel: 702-385 4011.* Dinner only. An excellent wine list complements this unexpected Downtown gem. The continental cuisine is a bit dated, but the experience is elegant and romantic.

The Buffet $ *Golden Nugget Hotel, tel: 702-385 7111.* Breakfast, lunch, and dinner. This is the buffet that set the modern standard. An elegant and comfortable dining room accommodates diners who choose from a huge variety of well-executed, all-you-can-eat fare.

Triple 7 Brewpub $ *Main Street Station, tel: 702-387 1896.* Open 11am–7am. The Triple 7 Brewpub is a virtually unknown (in Las Vegas) delight. Ales and beers brewed on the premises complement a fresh and innovative menu of American and Asian cuisine, as well as delicious wood-fired pizzas.

OFF-STRIP RESTAURANTS

Benihana Village $$ *Las Vegas Hilton, tel: 702-732 5111.* Dinner only. The same Benihana experience you may have had in other US cities: an Asian eatery set in an elaborate garden. Energetic chefs entertain by cooking Japanese food in front of the diners.

Carnival World Buffet $ *Rio All-Suites Hotel and Casino, tel: 702-252 7757.* Breakfast, lunch, and dinner. The main attractions here are the numerous cooked-to-order food stations ranging from Asian to Mexican to Italian. The buffet combines a fresh-food approach with the mass-audience aesthetic.

Chicago Joe's $–$$ *820 South 4th Street, tel: 702-382 5637.* Lunch and dinner. A tiny restaurant in a former Downtown home, Joe's has been serving tasty southern Italian pastas and shellfish for over 20 years.

Dona Maria Tamales Restaurant $ *910 Las Vegas Boulevard South, tel: 702-382 6538.* Lunch and dinner. Dona Maria's is an authentic Mexican restaurant, specializing in tamales. The choice is a wide one: choose from hot pork, mild chicken, or chile-and-cheese varieties.

The Feast Buffet $ *Palace Station, tel: 702-367 2411.* The innovator of a modern buffet trend, the Feast was responsible for the live-action cooking now found in buffets citywide. Made-to-order omelets, multiple ethnic food stations, and a smorgasbord of desserts make this one of the best buffet bargains in town.

Golden Steer Steakhouse $$$ *308 West Sahara Avenue, tel: 702-384 4470.* The Golden Steer is *the* classic Vegas steakhouse; it has the atmosphere of a bordello. If you like big steaks served in dark booths, you'll love this place.

Hamada of Japan $$ *598 East Flamingo Road, tel: 702-733 3005.* A lounge, sushi bar, and dining room combine to make this a major Japanese food experience. A favorite meal-time diversion is to watch your own food being cooked at the *hibachi* tables.

Jazzed Café and Vinoteca $ *2055 East Tropicana Avenue, tel: 702-798 5995.* Dinner and late-night dining. This tiny, elegant, candle-lit cafe serves carefully crafted Tuscan specialties–risotto, pastas, and salads–complemented by an extensive wine list. Best of all, it is open until about 4am.

Lindo Michoacan $$ *2655 East Desert Inn Road, tel: 702-735 6828.* Lunch and dinner. This authentic Mexican restaurant serves elaborate south-of-the-border cuisine. Specialties include wonderful roasted goat meat that is served with rich sauces and freshly-made flour tortillas.

Mama Marie's Cucina $$ *Rio All-Suites Hotel and Casino, tel: 702-247 7926.* Lunch and dinner. Continuing the Rio tradition, Mama Marie's serves good pasta dishes and breads at reasonable prices. You'll like the casual atmosphere as well.

Mr Lucky's 24/7 $ *Hard Rock Hotel, tel: 702-693 5000.* Mr Lucky's is an 'always open' hotel restaurant that breaks the mold. In other words, it's not shabby and down-at-the-heels, but instead is nicely decorated and has a welcomingly festive atmosphere. The menu offers standard American classics such as hamburgers, steak, pizza, and pasta.

Mortoni's $$ *Hard Rock Hotel, tel: 702-693 5047.* Dinner only. Mortoni's has Italian specialties as well as thick, juicy steaks served in an atmosphere of sublime elegance. Ask for outdoor seating if the weather is good.

Papamios $$ *Sam's Town Hotel and Casino, tel: 702-456 7777.* Dinner only. A surprisingly elegant Italian restaurant in a library-like setting. The pastas are very good, and the entrees excellent. 'Outdoor' dining is available under the atrium.

Napa Restaurant $$$$ *Rio All-Suites Hotel and Casino, tel: 702-247 7961.* Dinner only. Some local gourmands consider Napa the finest restaurant in the state. The decidedly upscale, country-French cooking brings nouvelle cuisine to Las Vegas in force. The wine list is superior, too.

Suzette's $$$$ *Santa Fe Hotel and Casino, tel: 702-658 4900.* Dinner only. Suzette's is a French gourmet restaurant that manages to lure visitors away from the Strip – no mean feat in this town. The steak tartar and lobster thermidor are particularly good.

The Voodoo Café $$ *Rio All-Suites Hotel and Casino, tel: 702-247 7800.* Lunch and dinner. High atop the Rio, with a view overlooking all of Las Vegas, enjoy spicy Creole and Cajun specialties, served in a somewhat-decadent atmosphere.

Z'Tejas $$ *3824 Paradise Road, tel: 702-732 1660.* Lunch and dinner. Z'Tejas has elevated Southwestern cooking to an art form. Appreciative diners enjoy jalapeno chicken pasta, vegetable enchiladas, and other spicy selections that are served in a modern, casually elegant atmosphere.

INDEX